SAVVY LEADERSHIP

A Woman's Guide to 21st Century Entrepreneurial Leadership

by

Dr. Millicent Gray Lownes-Jackson

Edited by Dr. Leah Grubbs

TM

BOOK DESIGN AND LAYOUT BY DESIGN VISUALIZATIONS
www.designvisualizations.com

*For permission to reprint articles appearing in this publication or to subscribe
to the column, "Entrepreneurially Yours," contact
Dr. Millicent Gray Lownes-Jackson at Success@womaninbiz.com*

*For information about additional publications and services available from
A Business of Your Own, visit www.abusinessofyourown.com*

Preface

CONGRATULATIONS!!!

By merely opening this publication you have taken one of the first steps toward developing the skills and leadership acumen to be a successful savvy entrepreneurial leader in the 21st Century.

Entrepreneurial ventures and entrepreneurial leaders come in all shapes and sizes. Are you an entrepreneurial leader who has had the vision and guts to start a business to satisfy an identified need in the marketplace, or are you an entrepreneurial leader who has a passion to address societal issues and has established a social entrepreneurial firm? Or, are you the "glue" and guiding force of any type of entrepreneurial organization who leads with guts, determination, vision, and creativity and may hold the title of CEO, COO, or Chief Cook and Bottle Washer? Regardless of the leadership title you may hold, or even may aspire to hold, this publication is for you. *SAVVY LEADERSHIP* is designed for entrepreneurs who desire to successfully lead entrepreneurial ventures in the 21st Century as well as for those who desire to have an in-depth understanding of the intricacies and peculiarities of operating an entrepreneurial venture so that they can be effective managers and leaders in entrepreneurial ventures.

SAVVY LEADERSHIP will equip you with the business knowledge and information necessary to successfully lead an entrepreneurial venture through the 21st Century. This publication consists of a compilation of articles from the author's business column that highlight crucial business knowledge, success tips, business resources, wisdom, and inspiration for savvy business development and business operations. Information is presented topically, in a "quick read" format. At the end of your reading, you will have identified the specific steps you need to take for developing and implementing your personal entrepreneurial leadership plan of action and have the knowledge, information, and inspiration to become a savvy entrepreneurial leader of the 21st Century.

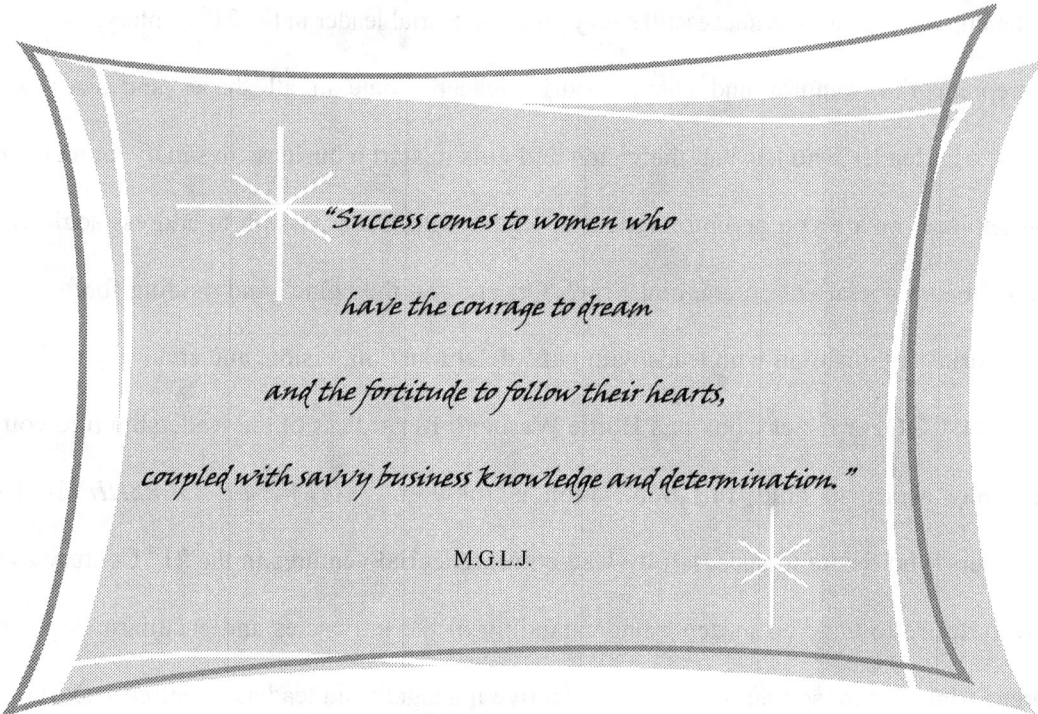

"Success comes to women who

have the courage to dream

and the fortitude to follow their hearts,

coupled with savvy business knowledge and determination."

M.G.L.J.

Table of Contents

Introduction

"The successful entrepreneurial leader

starts with a vision and

passionately details a plan to bring the vision to fruition."

M.G.L.J.

Patty cake, patty cake, baker's man, make me a husband as fast as you can, will he be a doctor, lawyer, or Indian chief.... and so goes the game that many women played as little girls. Today it's different. Women don't have to worry about the career of their spouse to determine their lifestyle. Women are successful doctors, lawyers, chiefs, rocket scientists, astronauts, and entrepreneurial leaders determining their own lifestyle and making their own impact on society and the nation's economy. In fact, women-owned businesses represent the fastest growing business sector of America's economy. The 21st Century is experiencing a new wave of entrepreneurial women leaders with a firey desire to put their initiative, creativity, and energy to work to realize a strong sense of personal worth, wealth, prestige, and a way of controlling one's own time and destiny while contributing to the nation's economic health and global competitiveness.

America's economic and entrepreneurial fabric changed significantly during the 20th Century. As we proceed in the 21st Century, global opportunities abound. Be it the former Soviet Union, South Africa, China, Afghanistan, or any other environment where we historically did not dare to even think about entrepreneurially, opportunities exist for the envisioned, aggressive entrepreneur.

With an internationally focused and a technologically advanced business sector, along with a more culturally diverse workforce, it can no longer be business as usual in America. Changes are occurring on every front; and to be successful, the "Millentrepreneurial" leader, the new millennium entrepreneurial leader, must be ready with the knowledge, skills, and information to be a savvy power broker.

Internationalism, technology, women-owned businesses, and diversity are obvious and commonly cited changes in America's way of doing business. But, even management techniques and business practices will continue to change in the 21st Century with the female managerial mystic moving front and center. Futurists predict that the 21st Century will experience increasing numbers of women rising to take their rightful positions on the throne of thriving entrepreneurial endeavors. Armed with an inherent, empowering, visionary leadership style which encourages participation, sharing power and information, getting others excited about their work, enhancing other people's self worth, providing a nourishing environment for growth, flexibility, creativity, pay for performance, team building, and consensus building, female-owned businesses are poised for development, growth, and expansion in the 21st Century.

The 21st Century business environment, driven by technological advances including the Internet, fax, cellular phone, e-mail, palm pilot, and video conferencing, has significantly evened the odds for small business. The entrepreneurial spirit is a driving force of the economic tapestry of the United States. In fact, new millennium entrepreneurial leaders, "Millentrepreneurial" leaders, are thriving in the hottest business industries. What are these industries? These industries, identified by futurists, trade groups, and professional surveys, include, but are not limited to, technology and telecommunications, medical, child and elder care, business consulting, transportation and tourism, and the arts. They also include the broad field of finance, specialized niches, such as catering, natural food products, and the traditional area of construction. A societal trend toward greater appreciation of the arts makes it also a great time for entrepreneurs to go venturing on the softer side of life. As we move into a truly global culture, the booming industries are those that are shaped by a world where boundaries are merely lines on a map. They are also industries that seem to make life easier for an increasingly affluent generation of twenty-somethings or aging baby boomers.

Futurists predict that in the 21st Century, some traditionally female professionals will gain new respect and prominence including nurses, teachers, and executive-level administrative assistants, all of whom also hold promise for entrepreneurial pursuits. And, from welfare reform, will also emerge many incredible entrepreneurs with proven track records of beating the odds and surviving adversity. They will hit the entrepreneurial trail with a level of strength, fortitude, motivation, and determination to succeed in entrepreneurship.

Regardless of the many new millennium opportunities that afford a chance to realize entrepreneurial dreams, there are nightmares and challenges along the road to entrepreneurial leadership success. Attaining capital, having insufficient profit, obtaining adequate sales, positioning in the market, affording health insurance, finding good employees, keeping up with technology, developing financial systems and controls, organizing processes, acquiring selling skills, managing stress, dealing with social inequities, securing government and corporate accounts, breaking the "ole boy" network, effectively and efficiently managing operating expenses, feeling isolated, managing time, and being able to trust key employees present challenges for the successful entrepreneur.

The Millentrepreneurial leader will also face new exciting and challenging economic trends that will significantly impact business success. The Millentrepreneurial leader, however, will experience many traditional challenges and expectations that entrepreneurs have experienced in the 20th Century and centuries past. A non-sensitization to these factors can quickly cause the demise of non-astute entrepreneurs.

New Millennium Economic Impactors

- **An Ever-Increasing Global Economy and Marketplace**

- **Increasing Diversity in America and its impact on Marketing and Personnel**

- **Changing Purchasing Habits of Consumers, i.e., e-business, TV**

- **Countries changing borders, politics, and economies**

- **New security issues as businesses and the country realize their vulnerability after 9-11**

- **Keeping up with High Technology**

- **Rapidly Changing Information and Telecommunication Technology**

- **Resurgence of Popularity of Entrepreneurs Working and Residing at the Same Address**

- **New legal issues of ownership: Limited Liability Company (LLC) and Limited Liability Partnership (LLP)**

- **Ever-Increasing Number of Women Business Owners**

Yes, entrepreneurial challenges exist on every front. The challenges, however, make the world of the entrepreneur intriguing, exciting, and financially rewarding when overcome with business savvy. While these 21st Century trends hold great promise for expanding opportunities for savvy entrepreneurial leaders, diminishing returns will be experienced by the non-astute. The 21st Century is the era for savvy leadership. It's the time to lead with vision, fortitude, determination, sound contemporary business and management knowledge, skills, and practices; and it's time to actuate others to assist in shared-vision accomplishment with style, class, grace, and sophistication.

Section I

SAVVY LEADERSHIP
FOR
THE 21ST CENTURY

THE ENTREPRENEURIAL LEADERSHIP CHALLENGE

*Entrepreneurial leadership is **a challenging, exhilarating, yet exhausting** way of life. The entrepreneurial leadership road to success is filled with **risk, problems,** and **pitfalls, but at the end of the road is the gleaming, vibrant light of success, and the thrill of accomplishment**.*

*The entrepreneurial leader **must meet the frustrations along the road with perseverance. Perseverance, continual planning,** and **hard work** enable the entrepreneurial leader to overcome the obstacles inherent in any venture.*

Like creating the intricate components of a computer system or cultivating a rose garden, pulling together all the elements of successful entrepreneurial leadership is an art that requires knowledge, skill, hard work, experience, and unwavering determination.

14

As we stand at the dawning of a new millennium, an era like no other we have ever seen before, it's an era where it is predicted by futurists that women will take their rightful seats on the throne as queens leading major corporations, leading the nation, and leading our major organizations. It's time, ladies, to revisit your leadership skills so that we are prepared to lead. The 21st Century is an era during which it is predicted that traditional, female-stereotyped fields like teaching and nursing will rise in prominence. It's an era where the "soft" people skills, being humanistic/compassionate, coaching, and nurturing, which in recent history were shunned because they were "female," will be the skills necessary to lead our organizations of every type to new horizons.

> *Savvy Leadership:* Leading with vision, getting others to see the vision, grounded with sound, contemporary business and management trends and principles, and leading with grace, class, and style.

It's time to get busy--busy building our organizations, our communities, our families, and our future. We have to be the ones to *LEAD*.

Look into the future with vision;

Empower others to assist in accomplishing the vision;

Actuate your followers with

Decisive action.

Ladies, we have to be the architects for change.

There are challenges on every front…

➢ Youth who are lost, disenchanted, with a sense of hopelessness
➢ Youth incarceration
➢ Babies having babies
➢ Drugs in our communities
➢ Crime in neighborhoods
➢ The struggling unemployed and underemployed
➢ Welfare instead of employment
➢ Health challenges including AIDS, heart disease, cancer, hypertension, and health insurance issues
➢ The education and mis-education of our children
➢ Economic, pay, and equity challenges
➢ And, the list goes on and on

And we face all of these challenges with an awe-inspiring backdrop of terrorism, an active war, and the fear of biological and chemical warfare.

Yes, it's a new era. It's time for strong leadership, and it's time to get busy. We must take the lead, and we must be savvy with our leadership. And what do I mean by Savvy Leadership? Taking the helm with vision, getting others to see the vision; empowering others to help in achieving the vision; and leading with grace, class, sophistication, and style. It's our time. And it's our time to have serious conversations about leadership.

Leadership: THE UNIQUE ABILITY TO GIVE PEOPLE THE DESIRE TO FOLLOW.

It's time to take the lead fortified with the savvy necessary for 21st Century success. What does the model for 21st Century entrepreneurial leadership encompass? It first starts with in-depth understanding of yourself, the leader. You must know who you are, your leadership style, and the style that works best in your operating environment.   After a thorough self-assessment, you next must focus on interpersonal relations and refine your relationship skills, your skills in motivating others, your communication skills, and your ability to develop a cohesive team desirous of pursuing the vision. Then, you must keep your attention on synergism and developing an organizational climate that encourages strategic planning, assessment of goal attainment, continuous organizational improvement, and receptiveness to making organization changes, as necessary, to accomplish the vision and the strategic plan.

Cardinal Rule of Leadership:

There is no leadership without "followship."

The following model depicts the components necessary for 21st Century leadership success.

A Model for 21st Century Savvy Leadership

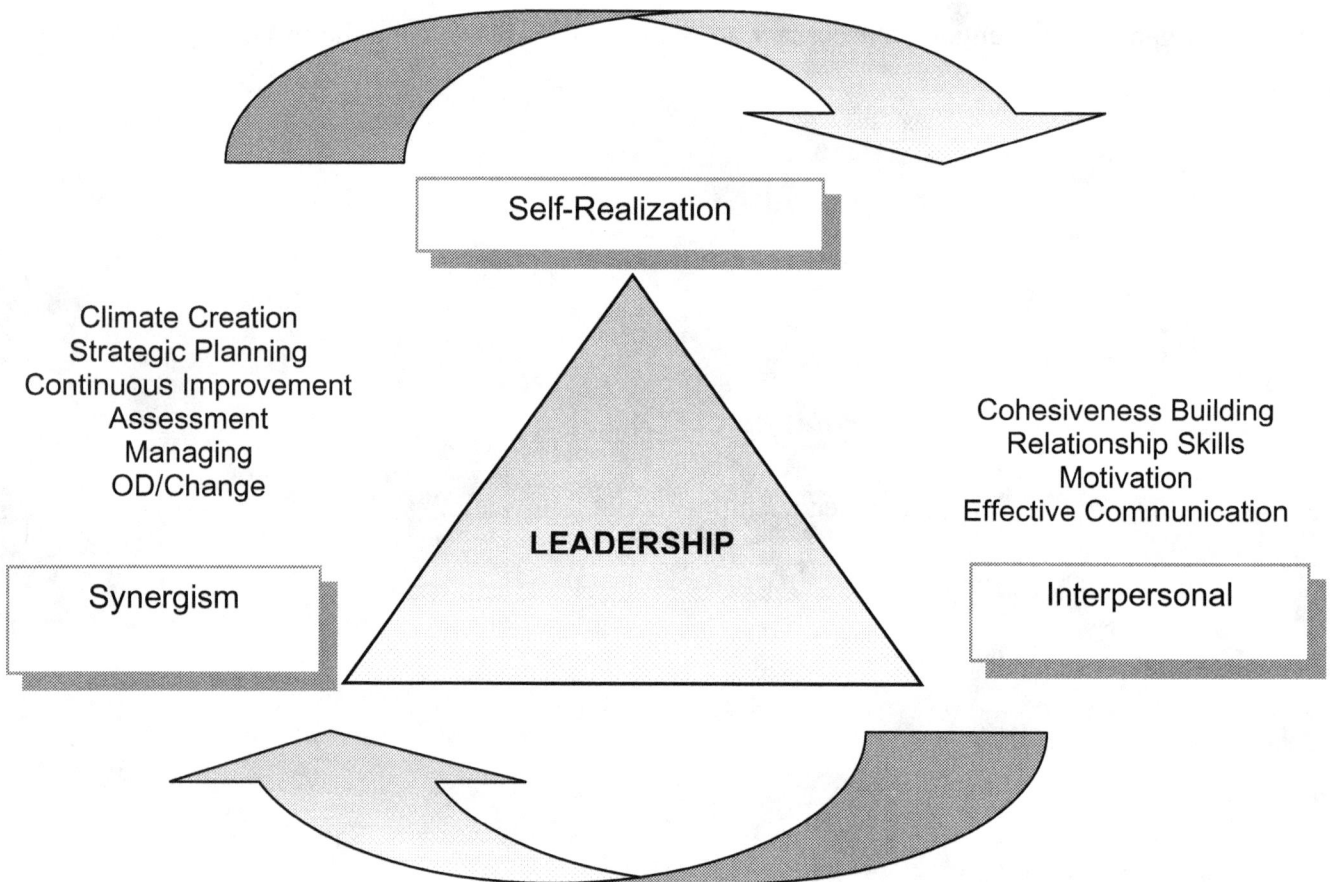

Self-Realization

Climate Creation
Strategic Planning
Continuous Improvement
Assessment
Managing
OD/Change

Cohesiveness Building
Relationship Skills
Motivation
Effective Communication

LEADERSHIP

Synergism

Interpersonal

Leadership Effectiveness depends on the leader, the people being led, and the organization context.

The successful entrepreneurial leader effectively implements the 21st Century leadership model with an understanding of the 21st Century business and management trends which include visionary leadership, integrity, accountability, respect, coaching, creative thinking, resiliency, continuous improvement and assessment, all in the context of the socio-economic environment within which they are operating.

The successful "Millentrepreneurial" leader must be a pillar of society and realize the importance of playing a major role in defining the immediate operating environment, the community. The foundation of any business is the character of the entrepreneurial leaders. We've all heard that the speed of the leader determines the speed of the pack. Well, the character of the leader determines the ethics of the company and ultimately the reputation of the business. The best business concept and business plan ever known to humanity will be fruitless if the entrepreneurial leader does not have strong morals and unwavering ethical practices. The entrepreneurial leader must be a person of character beyond reproach.

> *"Anybody wrapped in himself or herself makes too small a package to make a difference."*
> Rev. Chestina Archibald

An Entrepreneurial Leader of Character Is...

C   **COMMUNITY CONSCIOUS** -- *A good citizen, does his or her share, helps the community, plays by the rules, and respects authority and the law*

H   **HONEST** -- *Ethical, moral*

A   **ANCHORED IN FAITH** -- *Rests on faith as the solid rock of his or her existence and guiding force*

R   **RESPONSIBLE** -- *Accountable, meets the demands of duty, pursues excellence, exercises self control*

A   **ACTIVE IN THE COMMUNITY** -- *Sees needs in the community and tries to solve problems*

C   **CARING** -- *Compassionate, kind, loving, considerate, and charitable*

T   **TRUSTWORTHY** -- *Lives with integrity, is reliable and loyal*

E   **EQUITABLE** -- *Fair and just and is impartial, listens, and is open to differing viewpoints*

R   **RESPECTABLE** -- *Values all persons, lives by the Golden Rule, respects the dignity, privacy, and freedom of others*

19

Entrepreneurial leaders come to the global business table from all walks of life and varied career paths. But entrepreneurial leadership success doesn't occur without critical personal characteristics: hard work, dedication, focus, and commitment. Regardless of whether you're coming from a job you hate or a job you love, from corporate life or public service; from community service or academia, from working in the home or unemployment, you need to assess your skills, abilities, talents, and strengths for entrepreneurship. We all have many attributes which could be very beneficial in the world of entrepreneurship, but many of these positive traits often go overlooked and unidentified. Your strong points could include special talents, knowledge, past experience, tenacity, determination, level headedness, standing up well under stress, good communication skills, creativity, artistry, etc. Take a moment and list all of your strengths.

LIST YOUR STRENGTHS
(Don't be modest)

Just as you may have many personality characteristics which could help you succeed as an entrepreneurial leader, you may also have weaknesses which could eventually lead to entrepreneurial demise. Some of these weaknesses include a tendency not to complete tasks you start, being more comfortable as a follower and disliking leadership responsibilities, being

gullible, or too kindhearted, hating to hurt someone else's feelings even though you suffer the

negative consequences, being unorganized, hating details, etc. Remember, some tendencies or

traits may not have been considered weaknesses before, but need to be examined now in light

of the immense personal requirements necessary for success as a business owner and

entrepreneurial leader. Now, take time to list all of your weaknesses.

LIST YOUR WEAKNESSES
(Own up to all of them.)

Numerous studies suggest that there are certain personal requirements or personality

characteristics which successful small business owner-managers seem to have in common.

One such study was conducted by a team of psychologists at Case Western Reserve University.

This study utilized tests, questionnaires, and in-depth interviews to examine characteristics of

chief executive officers of several successful small businesses. The study resulted in the

following profile of the successful entrepreneur:[1]

1. The successful entrepreneur is a moderate risk taker--not a gambler. He [or she] is an adventurer.

2. The successful small business person is decisive and tends to like tight control over decision making.

3. The successful small business person is versatile and tends to strive for competence in many business areas.

4. The successful small business person is a finisher. He [or she] tends to have strong motives to achieve and endure until the completion of a task.

5. The successful small business person is self-confident. He [or she] has a strong belief in his [or her] own capabilities.

6. The successful business person is a benevolent despot, and he [or she] tends to be friendly and willing to listen to the suggestions of subordinates.

Another study of personality characteristics that lead to success in small business was made by H. B. Pickle. He identifies five characteristics he considers significant.[2]

1. Drive--comprised of responsibility, vigor, initiative, persistence, and health;

2. Thinking Ability--comprised of original or creative analytical thinking;

3. Human Relations Ability—comprised of ascendancy, emotional stability, sociability, cautiousness, consideration, cheerfulness, cooperation, and tact;

4. Communications Ability--both oral and written; and

5. Technical Knowledge--comprised of acquired skills developed through study and practical application.

A review of the literature on small business initiation, ownership, and management leads to the conclusion that there are various personal attributes necessary for success in entrepreneurship. The Small Business Administration (SBA), the governmental agency which assists small businesses, identifies certain personal attributes as being necessary for entrepreneurial success. Included in the list are the following 18 characteristics and abilities:

- *Understanding of others,*

- *Willingness to take a chance,*

- *Ability to withstand stress,*

- *Selling skills,*

- *Spirit to meet competition,*

- *High capability for organizing,*

- *Ability to adapt to change,*

- *Innovativeness,*

- *Honesty in business relationships,*

- *Initiative and leadership abilities,*

- *Ability to take over when the going gets rough,*

- *Ability to keep abreast of new technology in the field, as well as environmental changes,*

- *Industriousness and capability to work long hours,*

- *Ability to make and guide accurate decisions,*

- *Perseverance (not discouraged by obstacles),*

- *Desire to get ahead with a high level of energy,*

- *Ability to understand customers and their desires, and*

- *Ability to inspire and direct or motivate[3]*

All of us have unique skills, abilities, and inabilities. An in-depth, self-evaluation process allows you to identify your strongest areas and focus on interests and abilities which can be channelled strategically and successfully into a business venture. This process is critical prior to starting a business and certainly a necessity for continuing or staying on course for your entrepreneurial journey. Now, take time and compare your strengths and weaknesses with the research findings as to the requirements necessary for entrepreneurial success.

Answer these critical questions: How do your strengths compare to common qualities of successful entrepreneurial leaders? Do you have significant weaknesses? If so, can most of them be positively changed? Do you think you really have what it takes for entrepreneurial leadership success?

Even if you realize that you may not have the personal qualities necessary for entrepreneurial leadership success, do not become discouraged. There are many entrepreneurial leadership success qualities that can be learned and developed. To achieve business and leadership success, other qualities can be obtained by joining with other individuals who have the skills, abilities, expertise, or characteristics that you may lack.

So you've envisioned yourself with an impressive title of President, CEO or COO. That unmentionable self-esteem is satisfied, and you're already passing out business cards, in your mind if not in reality. But, the truth of the matter is, in the world of entrepreneurial leadership, you also hold the titles of vice president of finance, vice president of marketing, supervisor, and chief "bottle washer," and floor sweeper. You're on the road to be a "hard core" entrepreneur, striving for success and doing it all by yourself or with the help of only one or two employees. You hear all of the success stories about those who make millions in business for themselves and have "umpteen" employees. But you're probably quietly wondering about the real story about entrepreneurship.

Well, the reality is, there are many joys in the world of entrepreneurship, but there are also many trials and tribulations. The vast majority of American business owners are solo entrepreneurs who are making their impact on the economy either alone or with one to three employees. These entrepreneurs are receiving personal rewards such as financial security, wealth, personal satisfaction, and a chance of controlling their destiny. At the same time, their empires, regardless of size, are a major force in the economy, helping to insure competition and providing approximately half of all jobs in America. However, along the road to entrepreneurial success and self-fulfilment, many trials, unforeseen problems and challenges will be encountered. Some can be overcome and some are overwhelming.

Betty Tompkins of the Washington, DC area had been dabbling in entrepreneurship for years. She and her neighbor came up with a bright idea that they were sure would make them wealthy enough to kiss the boss goodbye. Betty, a public school speech pathologist, and her government official neighbor stepped out on faith with a plan to market homemade delicacies as a sideline business. Orders were coming in faster than they had ever anticipated. They quickly moved from a home-based operation to a commercial cooking facility. But the factors they didn't consider were the enormous costs of insurance and the inordinate amount of their time and energy that would be required to maintain a profitable level of operation. Just like Betty and her neighbor, unanticipated trials and tribulations of all types and magnitude impact entrepreneurs with great intentions.

On the personal side, there are drawbacks to success to consider. You may run into the double bind of taking so much of your time to make your business a success that when you realize the fruits of your labor and have extra money to enjoy life, you don't have time to really enjoy yourself. You may find that you have to constantly devote more time to keeping the business successful, and/or you find that your mind is constantly on the business. And yes, you may even need to consider subconscious jealousy and/or competition from your spouse or significant other and the negative repercussions.

Oh, the sweet, sweet joy of entrepreneurial success is certainly *good*. But, don't be unrealistic and overlook the *bad* and the *ugly.*

Given the many challenges, tribulations, and pitfalls of small business, the failure rate of small businesses is extraordinarily high. Reports indicate that as many as nine out of ten failures are traceable to managerial inexperience and incompetence. Other reasons for business failures include too little capital, poor organization, obsolescence of product, obsolescence of machinery, poor personnel practices, and inappropriate personal characteristics. General trials and tribulations encountered by entrepreneurs include the **Dangerous Dozen,** those lurking "animals" that are can cause business failure if you let your savvy leadership skills take a vacation for even a split second.

Beware of the Dangerous Dozen

1. *Lack of Management Knowledge and Experience*
2. *Lack of a Business Plan*
3. *Lack of Sufficient Capital*
4. *Poor Financial Management and Record Keeping*
5. *Taking Customers for Granted*
6. *Failure to Develop Employees and Teamwork*
7. *Failure to Keep Abreast of Industry, Environmental, Technological, and Global Changes*
8. *Lack of a Marketing Plan and Marketing Research*
9. *Becoming "Business Consumed"/ Egomania*
10. *Poor Stress and Time Management*
11. *Lack of Long-Range Planning and Unplanned Growth and Expansion*
12. *Wrong Location*

Business ownership offers for many a feeling of personal worth, wealth, prestige, and a way of controlling their own time and destiny. It offers a chance to be a **star,** but one must be prepared for the **wars** necessary to beat the **Dangerous Dozen**.

If you are serious about being in business, you need to stay in the know! For starters, develop a support system of people who are in business and of people who have their fingers on the pulse of what's happening in the community before it happens. Also consider becoming active in community organizations and the local Chamber of Commerce to stay on the right information vine. Get on the mailing list of associations pertaining to the nature of your business and local small business assistance agencies, as well as community groups and universities so that you will be informed about workshops and seminars. Not only do these programs provide valuable information, which many times is free, but they also are a good way to network and to further develop your information vine.

The entrepreneurial leader needs to seek out as much industry and environmental information as possible from primary and secondary information vines or printed materials. It is crucial to keep abreast of current and future industry trends as well as general economic and environmental changes.

If you're like most entrepreneurial leaders, you are focussed on action and making things happen so that your business will be successful. You don't even want to think about being still and spending time in a library to do research. However, many valuable resources can be found in the public library and on the Internet.

The information vine of secondary sources is entwined with a multitude of information to keep your business going and growing. In addition to the Internet and most familiar library sources such as the card catalog, business databases, <u>Reader's Guide to Periodical</u>

<u>Literature</u>, and general business publications such as the Wall Street Journal and Fortune, the following sources are highlighted as short cuts to obtaining the "right" information quickly.

LITERARY RESOURCES

BUSINESS PERIODICAL INDEX
(Subject index to English language periodicals. Also has an author listing of citations to book reviews)

STANDARD AND POOR'S INDUSTRY SURVEYS
(A comprehensive reference book divided into segments consisting of Basic and Current Analyses covering all major domestic industries)

"The only place success comes before work is in the dictionary."

Anonymous

DUNN AND BRADSTREET
(Contains the names and ratings of nearly 3 million businesses of all types located throughout the U.S. and Canada)

ULRICH'S INTERNATIONAL PERIODICALS DIRECTORY
(Lists magazine and trade publications for different types of businesses)

ENCYCLOPEDIA OF ASSOCIATIONS
(Lists organizations for different types of businesses)

JOURNAL OF COMMERCIAL BANK LENDING
(Contains periodic articles about different types of businesses)

THE THOMAS REGISTER
(A purchasing guide listing names of manufacturers, producers, and similar sources of supply in all lines)

DIRECTORY OF WHOLESALERS AND MANUFACTURERS
(Information on wholesalers, manufacturers and manufacturers' representatives of toys, games, hobby, art, school, party, and office-supply products under seven product headings)

GENERAL PERIODICALS
BUSINESS WEEK, INC., FORTUNE, IN BUSINESS, U.S. NEWS AND WORLD REPORT, NEWSWEEK, SUCCESS, TIME, BARRON'S, FORBES, BLACK ENTERPRISE, WALL STREET JOURNAL, NEW YORK TIMES, MONEY, BUSINESS 2.0, WIRED, ETC.

Section II

3 Ps of Entrepreneurial Success:

Planning, Passion, and Perseverance

"Three Critical Keys to Entrepreneurial Success:

PASSION, PLANNING, AND PERSEVERANCE."

M.G.L.J.

The Business Plan is a crucial ingredient for the success of any venture. For the firm that is already operating, *the Business Plan* serves as a guidepost for operating and strategic planning. For someone thinking about starting a business, *the Business Plan* will help structure thoughts and aid in determining the chances for the business to become a success prior to investing many dollars. Any lender or potential business supporter, including marketing and other consultants, expects business owners to have a clear concept of what they are doing and where they are trying to go. The Business Plan tells it all in an organized, coherent format.

A business plan is a report written by you about your venture at a particular point in time. Your business plan should describe your venture: **WHAT** it is, **WHO** will be active in it, **WHY** you believe it will be successful, and **HOW** you intend to implement your plans. It should be a concise, readable, well-written document. It should anticipate setbacks as well as success. And it should be dated, because you will want to revise or rewrite it at different times during the evolution of your business.

A business plan helps you stay on course. It is crucial to the internal operations of the business, as it serves as a checklist and timetable for accomplishing stated objectives. Additionally, it is essential in attracting external resources, both financial and human.

A thorough business plan should include clear descriptions and evaluatory remarks pertaining to the following indicated areas.

The Business

- Detailed description of the business, including name, location, business goals and objectives, industry information and assessment, economic trends, etc.;

- Description of the product (services and/or goods), potential of product line, technology, and possible advances;

- Description of the marketing plan, including target market, marketing strategies, channels of distribution, market size and share, market potential, pricing strategy, and promotion;

- Assessment of the competition;

- Management, covering such areas as key personnel, names of accountants, lawyers, consultants, organizational structure, experience of key personnel, educational background and experience;

- Legal structure, describing the proprietorship, partnership, or corporation;

- Personnel, listing personnel requirements, position descriptions, labor trends, and compensation;

- Facilities and equipment;

- Sources of supply;

- Critical risks and problems;

- Economic trends; and

- Strategies for the future.

Financial Data

- Capital equipment,

- Sources of funds,

- Balance sheet,

- Break-even analysis,

- Income projections or profit-loss statement,

- Pro forma cash flow,

- Uses of funds, and

- Desired funding.

Supporting Documents

- Resumes of key personnel,

- Personal financial statements,

- Credit reports,

- Letters of reference,

- Copies of leases,

- Contracts,

- Legal documents,

- Drawings,

- Photographs,

- Articles, and

- Any additional pertinent information.

"The best business plan ever written becomes futile effort if there is no execution. You must be prepared to "get off of go."

M.G.L.J.

Planning doesn't stop with the initial development of the business plan. It is a continuous, ongoing process that must take into consideration market shifts, economic trends, and changes in the competitive environment. The business owner must continuously assess the overall business situation and utilize the information to plan strategically for the future success of the business.

Business ownership is a challenging, exhilarating, yet exhausting way of life. The road to business success is filled with risks, problems, and pitfalls. The business owner must meet these frustrations with perseverance. Continual planning, hard work, and perseverance enable the business owner to overcome the obstacles inherent in any new venture.

Identify your passion, turn your passion into a profitable venture through planning, and, above all, persevere to create a business of your own that fulfills your dreams for the future.

On the next page, an outline of a basic business plan is given.

BUSINESS PLAN OUTLINE

THE BUSINESS

  a. DETAILED DESCRIPTION OF BUSINESS, INCLUDING
     STATEMENT OF PURPOSE ALONG WITH PRODUCTS /SERVICES
  b. INDUSTRY INFORMATION AND ECONOMIC TRENDS
  c. MARKET INFORMATION
  d. THE COMPETITION
  e. MARKETING PLAN
  f. PERSONNEL
  g. MANAGEMENT AND ORGANIZATION PLAN
     AND STRUCTURE
  h. LEGAL STRUCTURE
  i. FINANCIAL PLAN
  j. OPERATING AND CONTROL SYSTEMS PLAN
  k. CRITICAL RISKS AND PROBLEMS
  l. GROWTH PLAN
  m. SUMMARY

The Business Plan Cover Page should include the following:

- Name of Business
- Name of Principals
- Address, Phone #,
- E-Mail Address
- Web site

The Business Plan should also include a **Table of Contents** and an **Executive Summary**.

FINANCIAL DATA

  n. SOURCES AND APPLICATIONS OF FUNDS
  o. CAPTIAL EQUIPMENT LIST
  p. BALANCE SHEET
  q. BREAK-EVEN ANALYSIS
  r. INCOME PROJECTIONS (PROFIT AND LOSS STATEMENTS)
  s. PRO-FORMA CASH FLOW
  t. DEVIATION ANALYSIS
  u. HISTORICAL FIANCIAL REPORTS FOR AN EXISTING BUSINESS

SUPPORTING DOCUMENTS

(PERSONAL RESUMES, PERSONAL FINANCIAL STATEMENTS, COST OF LIVING, CREDIT REPORTS. LETTERS OF REFERENCE, LETTERS OF INTENT, CONTRACTS, LEGAL DOCUMENTS, LEASE AGREEMENTS, ETC.)

In addition to the business plan, in marketing businesses to government and corporate arenas, a document often requested is THE CAPABILITY STATEMENT. This document is a capsulated view of a firm's capabilities, experiences, and areas of expertise, as well as an inclusion of a listing of firms and government agencies who have believed in and utilized a firm's services and will attest to the firm's capabilities.

The Capability Statement, generally much briefer and more focussed on abilities than the business plan, includes the following major components:

Major Components of the Capability Statement

- Cover Sheet (Includes the firm's name, principals involved, address, phone number, e-mail address, certifications, and date)
- General Overview of the Firm and Services
- Delineation of Services the Firm is Capable of Providing to Varied Sectors
- Certificates and Qualifications
- Organization Structure
- Areas of Expertise
- Clients and References
- Qualification Statements (projects performed)
- Management Approach
- Staff and Support Resources

As the term implies, the capability statement, cuts through superficial, wordy, traditional marketing fluff, and gets to the bottom line: What the firm actually is capable of doing.

Futurists predict that home-based businesses will strongly continue their popularity in the 21st Century. Largely due to corporate downsizing coupled with telecommunications advances and societal changes, doing business at home--an old-fashioned way of conducting business-- is quickly becoming the new wave for the new age.

Women seem to be leading in the home-based business economy with varied reports showing that women own the majority of America's home-based businesses. Home-based businesses, however, seem to be attractive to all types of individuals, be they displaced professionals, homemakers, hobbyists, retirees, divorcees, young singles, disabled individuals, or the "sideline" entrepreneur. Many are looking for a second income; others are using their businesses as their main means of livelihood.

Home-based businesses offer the advantage of convenience, lower start-up costs, flexibility in terms of time and juggling other responsibilities, tax advantages for in-home business deductions, and low overhead, while still affording the benefits of being one's own boss. Disadvantages, however, include isolation, temptations that divert one's attention, interruptions from family and friends, space limitations, and difficulty in obtaining outside funding.

All types of businesses can be found operating from the home. The "New Age Cottage Industry" is much, much more than crafts and interior design services. It's business and technology products and services for the future. The Internet has done much to advance the status of the home-based business sector of our economy. Browsing the World Wide Web, one can find just about any product or service imaginable offered by a home-based business, including services to assist other home-based businesses.

Home-based businesses historically have experienced serious problems being recognized as full-fledged or legitimate businesses. Times are changing quickly, thanks particularly to the Internet, and the new wave of home-based "businessing" not only is viewed as credible but also offers many new and challenging opportunities for those with entrepreneurial savvy for the new age.

I bet you never thought of a business being an egg. But if a business is just getting started or is trying to expand, it in fact can be likened to an egg--a fragile egg that needs to be nurtured and developed so that it can hatch the right way at the right time and be ready for surviving in the globally competitive business world.

A concept that increasingly is spreading nationwide to assist in the incubation process of these fragile eggs--new and expanding businesses--Business Incubators. Incubation centers have been around for about 25 years but have only recently begun to enjoy a great surge in popularity with over 300 incubators located in 40 states.

But what is this thing called an incubator? Webster defines one type of incubator as one that serves as a preserving environment while the chicks are developing for their role in the outside world. Similarly, the small business incubator (sometimes called an innovation center) helps in the preservation of start-up enterprises by blunting the financial and experience problems new enterprises often encounter, while making available a pool of resources, including highly skilled consultants. An incubation center proposes to create an environment where small firms can "incubate" or grow and develop to a survivable size. The concept revolves around the provision of space, business consultation, and support services for small businesses which are just getting started, thereby allowing embryonic and infant small businesses to grow or incubate free of the initial high cost of infrastructure and with the provision of certain technical and Research and Development services. Research shows that 80 percent of companies nurtured in incubators survive compared to an 80 percent or more failure rate of new small businesses in general after five years.

As dissimilar as entrepreneurs and their types of ventures are, so are incubation centers and the services they offer. In fact, there is even variance in the nomenclature. Some view the term "incubation center" as being baby talk and offensive to center inhabitants. Terms such as technology centers, enterprise villages, entrepreneurial development centers, and innovation centers are common names for the same basic concept.

No two incubation centers are alike. They range from 20,000 to 1.5 million square feet in size; they usually occupy buildings, from schools to idled textile plants to abandoned railroad property. Sometimes, however, new facilities are established, such as pre-fabricated warehouses structures.

Some centers are initiated by local governments; others, by non-profit organizations or by universities who use the centers as a training ground for students. Still others are established by corporations or private developers who see a chance to make a profit, while at the same time, helping the community.

Similarly, funds may come from private sources, venture capitalists, foundations, or local, state, or federal governments, or universities. The co-location of entrepreneurs helps assure the cost-effective delivery of service and acts as a focal point for management assistance and on-going tenant networking. Services and facilities may include administrative and secretarial activities, a receptionist, an answering service, conference rooms, computer resources, photocopying, audio/visual equipment, warehousing, shipping, receiving, group purchasing opportunities, and on-site access to a wide range of business consultants. Additionally, some centers offer foreign trade assistance, technology transfer, access to university resources, and access to venture capital funds.

Despite its many advantages, however, the business incubator is not a panacea for all the difficulties a small business might experience during the developmental and expansion stages. Nevertheless, if your business is an egg in need of a warm, comfortable, controlled environment to develop, hatch, and grow, you may want to investigate incubation facilities in your area. The National Incubation Association keeps up-to-date information about incubation center locations across the country where firms can be nurtured.

The following words of wisdom are offered for reference for entrepreneurial leaders.

Business Plan	A document prepared by a business owner; it details specific, relevant information about the firm.
Entrepreneur	A person who organizes, manages, and initiates a business venture.
Mission	The long-term vision of what the firm is trying to become.
Objectives	The desired results for the company and its parts.
Retailer	A merchant or agent whose main business is to buy goods for resale to the ultimate consumer.
SBA	The Small Business Administration. The SBA is the major governmental agency formulated to assist small businesses.
SBDC	Small Business Development Center. SBDCs are established to provide free management assistance to small businesses.
Service Business	A firm filling non-goods needs of customers. Examples are child care centers, repair services, and physicians.
Strategy	A plan of action to attain objectives.
Strategic Plan	A major, comprehensive, long-term plan providing direction for a firm to accomplish its mission and objectives.
Trade Association	An organization formed to benefit members of the same trade by informing and supporting its members.

Section III

THE MANAGERIAL CHALLENGE

"Successful entrepreneurial leaders are intuitive,

display integrity in all of their actions,

and approach challenging situations with ingenuity."

M.G.L.J.

You've dreamed, you've planned, and you've persevered to get your business where it is today. Be it that the business is just getting off the ground or already has a progressive track record, keeping the business going and growing requires strategic macro and micro planning and good management practices. Macro planning occurs initially with the development of the business plan when you focus on how to implement plans for your business venture. Most business plans, however, overlook the minute details related to micro planning or internal planning, objective formulation, and managing day-to-day operations.

> **THE SPEED OF THE ENTREPRENEURIAL LEADER DETERMINES THE PACE OF THE ORGANIZATION**
> M.G.L.J.

As many as 80 percent of small business failures are attributed to poor management. Most people, however, think management means simply managing employees. This is an aspect of management, but management involves much, much more. Management involves planning and establishing objectives and/or goals for every aspect of the business. It encompasses structuring and organizing, and often re-organizing the business, to accomplish those objectives while at the same time providing strong leadership that can motivate employees to actually achieve what is desired. All of this falls apart if the entrepreneur doesn't also have good controls to ensure that objectives are in fact accomplished.

Internal planning and the formulation of sound objectives, coupled with an effective management style, are the key cornerstones to effective and efficient operations and is often where ambitious entrepreneurs get off base. All too often entrepreneurs are so consumed with obtaining business in order to make money and meet the payroll that they lose sight of the importance of their internal operations.

It is recommended that firms have objectives in the following areas:

- *Desired Market Share*
- *Innovation*
- *Productivity*
- *Physical and Financial Resources*

- *Profit*
- *Manager Performance and Development*
- *Worker Performance and Attitude*
- *Community Service*

Having well-founded objectives in these areas will not mean a thing if the entrepreneur does not share them with employees and motivate employees to accomplish them. Based on your particular employee base, it is advisable to get employees involved in helping to determine appropriate organizational objectives so that they will be more committed to their accomplishment. But having objectives and commitment are not enough; there needs to be a concrete strategic plan with detailed action steps developed for accomplishing all objectives. Then good management, the guiding force, comes into play to make sure the plans are followed and objectives are actually achieved.

Regardless of the size of your business venture, there is a need for some systematic way of doing things or some form of organization. A good way of approaching organizational structure is to consider all the activities necessary to accomplish the objectives of the firm. Categorize or sort these activities into feasible groupings, and establish appropriate authority for each classification. The entrepreneurial leader must thoroughly define the personnel required for the accomplishment of the activities of each grouping, prepare an organizational chart, and then thoroughly re-examine all activities and groupings for efficiency and effectiveness.

Such a procedure involves delegation of authority and responsibility. Delegation itself is often difficult for the entrepreneur because it involves letting loose of part of the decision making and some control. But proper delegation of authority is necessary for success. One of the main keys to effective delegation is knowing what to delegate and having competent and reliable employees to whom to delegate. With the delegation of authority goes the assignment of responsibility for the completion of the

> *Effective leaders give their followers enough authority to carry out assigned tasks.*

delegated tasks. However, accountability cannot be delegated. The entrepreneur is responsible for the successful operation of the firm, and how successfully the delegated tasks are accomplished will still fall back on the business owner's shoulders. So the importance of competent employees is evident along with the necessity for a formalized system of control.

For guidance, basic organizing principles and structure formats follow.

Basic Organizing Principles

1. Unity of Command

Employees should have only one superior to whom they are directly responsible.

2. Parity of Authority

Authority should be equal with responsibility. When delegating responsibility, measures must be taken to make sure employees have enough authority to carry out their duties and responsibilities, but not more authority than necessary. Be sure employees have a written statement of their duties, authority, responsibilities, and relationships.

Ways of Organizing Your Business

There are several common ways of structuring a business which include organizing by the following methods:

- **Function:** *similar skills are grouped to form a functional unit such as production or marketing.*

- **Product:** *the business is structured according to the individual products offered to the public.*

- **Process:** *similar processes, such as welding or painting, are the basis for organizing the firm.*

- **Geographic area:** *some firms have locations in different geographical areas and are organized primarily on the basis of territorial concerns.*

- **Type of customers serviced:** *some firms service different types of customers, such as retail or wholesale customers, and are structured accordingly.*

- **Project:** *some firms, such as consulting businesses, are organized internally based on projects being researched or directed.*

- **Individual talents of subordinates:** *some organizations are structured based on the particular areas of expertise of employees.*

"Letting go" is probably one of the hardest lessons for entrepreneurs to learn. "Letting go" means delegating duties and activities to others to perform. When it"s your baby, your dream and your vision, it's so very difficult to entrust others with the responsibility to make varied aspects of your business work.

Entrepreneurs, in general, don't delegate for many reasons. Some of the reasons include fear of losing control, the desire for perfectionism, the belief that delegating takes more time than doing it yourself, the general compulsion to be involved in all aspects of the business, lack of faith in employees' abilities, as well as the concern that employees may learn so much that they will eventually leave and start their own business. But delegation is crucial if the business is to grow.

An Effective Entrepreneurial Leader has the intelligence to select good team members to assist in getting the job done and the self-restraint to keep from meddling with them while they do it.

M.G.L.J.

Delegation is a science in itself which involves careful thought and execution. It involves hiring right and firing right and coming to grips with which aspects of the business you feel comfortable in delegating. When delegating, not only do you need to select individuals well suited for the delegated tasks, but you also need to set clear performance criteria and guidelines, a schedule for progress reports and completion, as well as provide the necessary resources and authority to actually fulfill your expectations.

With delegating, everything may not be done your way, but business can still run smoothly. Accepting and acknowledging that people and their approaches may vary from yours but still bring about good--or even better results--is all part of letting go. Delegation removes some of the day-to-day stress and allows you the opportunity to keep focused on opportunities and the broader picture as well as gives employees a chance to learn and grow.

But this can only happen if you just learn to "let go."

Putting out fires is a way of life for the entrepreneurial leader. Faced constantly with problems of varying dimensions and magnitudes, learning to put out fires effectively and permanently is a crucial managerial skill for entrepreneurial success.

Entrepreneurial demands can be overwhelming. With limited time and an overabundance of stress, entrepreneurs are tempted to deal with the most pressing problem or situation as quickly as possible, or sometimes not at all if they think it will go away. The truth of the matter is that the same problem will be encountered over and over if the core of the problem is never attacked.

Although becoming a good problem solver takes much experience, there are some basic thoughts that should prove to be helpful. When faced with a situation, take time to evaluate it in terms of what the most desired situation is compared to the present situation at hand. Next, identify what is causing the desired situation not to be the actual situation, Sure, this sounds academic; but this is how you start cutting through superficial clouds and emotional overtones surrounding real problems. In other words, you begin to get to the source of the problem versus taking action to simply eliminate symptoms. Only after you have a clear picture of the core of the problem can varying ways to solve the problem be identified. No, this approach does not necessarily require a pen and paper nor hours of intellectual assessment. It involves incorporating a problem-solving approach to situations in your common-sense, business-operating base. Once this occurs, you can still put out all the fires you need to on the spot; but the way you put them out, going all the way to the core, will also put out all of the hot spots and leave no embers smoldering.

America's work force is changing right before our eyes. As more minorities and non-American born employees join the work force, coupled with an aging work population, and a concern for the handicapped, it will be the companies that manage diversity who will come out ahead in the 21st Century's very globally competitive environment.

The days of "when I see you, I see no color," are over. Diversity astuteness means you see color and differences and respect and understand those differences. It is crucial for these diverse groups to work and live in harmony, recognizing and appreciating differences and breaking prejudice and stereotypical barriers that all of us, as humans, have.

Organizations must accommodate the needs of all workers if they are to have a stable work force and retain their competitiveness in the cut-throat world of global concerns. Progressive firms are implementing diversity plans. A good diversity plan first encompasses a diversity audit assessing the extent of a firm's diversity in terms of race, ethnic background, sex, age, weight, sexual preferences, religious preferences, cultural background, and disabilities. The audit should identify any problems or concern areas presently existing. This is followed by a strategic action plan including sensitivity training, designing a coaching-monitoring program for all employees, and creating a climate that supports diversity.

Cultural diversity is not just race or ethnic background. It's much, much more. It needs to be understood, recognized, valued, and effectively managed. If American business is to recover lost productivity and regain its competitive edge in the 21st Century with a renewed sense of preeminence, it will have to effectively attract and manage the diverse talent that characterizes its new work force.

The family-owned business is much, much more than just a business. It is an enterprise consisting of a group of individuals who all share one of the strongest relationships humans can have...family bonds. In addition to the normal stress that comes with trying to make a business successful, family businesses also experience the strains of a family ranging from sibling rivalries to conflict between parents and children and husbands and wives.

In the family-owned business, business decisions are highly influenced by feelings about and responsibilities toward relatives. The normal management problems in the family-owned firm are thus greatly complicated by emotional family ties. Very few people have a family tree consisting entirely of people you want to be with five, six, or seven days out of the week for the majority of the day. So with family members in the business, just as with any employee group, there will be problems and disputes. When family members are involved, we tend to call the problems "a little conflict." Whatever you wish to call it, there will be hassles with the family tree business participants. Complaints are often heard such as the parent never stops treating the child as a child and about husbands exerting traditional male values and philosophies related to the business role of the wife. But for many, working together, particularly husband and wife teams, can offer a relationship greater substance. By being in business together, the family members have common interests and goals and more to discuss, thus keeping communication open in the relationship and making their bond even stronger.

The wise family business owner will plan in advance for the dismal possibility of family disputes, break ups, divorce, and the death of key family business members. Written agreements should be developed before such negative situations occur when emotions are not running high. With consultation from your attorney, accountant, and financial planner, agreements should be prepared for all potential problem areas as well as for succession.

For the "successors to the throne" of the family business that also has non-family employees, there are unique problems including resentment on the part of non-family and family members and problems related to establishing credibility. The most insignificant mistake on the part of the successor is often perceived as incompetency versus an error. It is suggested that "successors to the throne" first obtain employment outside the firm. This is suggested because it allows the young successor a chance to obtain a level of personal accomplishment, self confidence, and independence as well as a broader perspective of the business world. Outside success can also win the young entrant into the family business instant credibility and respect upon joining the firm. The recommended ideal situation is to groom those family members you wish to become involved in the business over a period of years. In fact, I recommend getting children involved in the business at a very early age. Children as young as 6 or 7 can do "little things" in the business. Additionally, you, the entrepreneurial parent, serve as an excellent role model for your children as you display qualities of being a hard worker and a business person with determination and the burning desire to achieve success. This type of exposure gives children a "common sense" business reference base which will help them in life in general, regardless of whether they take on roles in the family business.

If you are looking for expansion opportunities for your business, you may want to consider marketing to the government as part of your business plan. Local, state, and federal governments all buy various commodities from small businesses. The products procured range in nature from paper clips and cosmetics to computers, heavy machinery, and consultation services.

Government agencies generally have a small business liaison person to help small firms in investigating the feasibility of marketing their products or services to their agency. The phone number for the small/disadvantaged business specialist of locally based government entities can usually be found by consulting the government listings in your telephone book. To obtain detailed information about procurement procedures for specific federal government departments, write or call the division of interest.

The U.S. Small Business Administration offers electronic database services developed to assist small businesses in their efforts to obtain a fair share of government procurement opportunities. You should contact your local office of the SBA for details or visit **www.sba.gov.**

And, you don't need big trucks or paving equipment to take advantage of contracts with the U.S. DOT which spends billions with firms certified as small and disadvantaged. The office has a Web site that lists opportunities in a variety of areas, such as Web page design, management training, or management consulting.

An important general government procurement information source is The <u>Commerce Business Daily</u> newspaper, available in most local libraries. This newspaper publishes notices of requests for proposals and bidding opportunities and is considered the "Bible" of federal contacting.

Government procurement opportunities can prove to be very lucrative, and recent developments help to ensure receipt of compensation on a more timely basis than has been true historically. Realize, however, it is not wise to rely on any government contract as the main revenue source for your business.

Whether you are arranging a meeting for your office staff, sales personnel, or a community organization, the following information is provided to assist in making your next meeting work for you.

1. CONSIDER IF THE MEETING IS REALLY NECESSARY

It is important to first objectively determine the purpose of the meeting you are considering and then assess if the purpose can adequately be accomplished without a meeting. Certainly, many meetings are necessary since the matters at hand require the input, interaction, and visual contact with several parties. However, many times a meeting is not really necessary to deal with a situation; and in fact you can often keep a group's momentum going better if you don't waste their time at an unnecessary gathering. Often, personal phone calls, private discussions, memos, notices on a bulletin board, or a simple conference call can allow you to accomplish your objectives.

Before convening a meeting, make sure you know exactly what you want to accomplish and take time to assess group dynamics that might impact your accomplishing your meeting objectives.

2. DETERMINE THE TRUE PURPOSE OF THE MEETING

If it is determined that a meeting is necessary, then it is time to determine who should attend. Here you need to consider the matters at hand, who is needed to accomplish your objectives, and the group dynamics. Consider the following:

- Why is each person being invited?

- How important is each person's expertise, interest, or knowledge related to the purpose?

- Are there possible personality or attitude problems?

3. STRATEGICALLY PLAN THE MEETING

In planning a meeting, determine the agenda and resource materials needed. If it is an on-going meeting situation, determine if minutes from the previous meeting should be sent to those invited, along with the agenda for the planned meeting. Before sending these materials, evaluate the group you are dealing with. Based on group dynamics, sometimes it is better not to let individuals know all past and future information in advance, as some groups have cliques that have nothing better to do than discuss items before the meeting. They often arrive with their own hidden agendas which will deter from your planned purpose.

Finally, make sure the meeting is held in a thought-conducive environment void of interruptions. Create the atmosphere you want and keep to your agenda. Start the meeting on time regardless of how many people are there; latecomers will be on time for the next meeting when they realize that your meetings start on time. End the meeting in a timely fashion and continually make sure the meeting is working for you.

Change is a certainty of life that makes many humans, if not most, uncomfortable. Change involves moving from the known to the unknown; and just as change is not comfortable in our personal lives, change is not comfortable in the business world.

Change in the business arena is referred to as organizational change and usually refers to a major organizational alteration such as restructuring an organization, changing an organization's mission and direction, the introduction of new technologies that impact the way of doing business, new program implementation, such as Total Quality Management (TQM), or downsizing or "rightsizing."

Usually organizational change is initiated due to some major provocation such as decreased revenue, a changing market, decrease in productivity, new management or ownership, a need to expand market share, etc. Whatever the reason for considering change, it should not be done merely for the sake of change. It should be a well-thought-out strategy to accomplish some overall goal.

In order to bring about successful change in any operating environment, the individuals at the top must be involved, individuals affected by the change should be involved, and strategies must be employed to prepare individuals and get them postured to be receptive to change. This encompasses open communication and helping employees see the need for change. It is advisable, where appropriate, to even have employees involved by providing input as to what changes are needed to bring about the desired results. This helps to counteract resistance to change and helps in avoiding internal morale problems along with the fact that it makes good savvy business sense to get input from those who are on the front line performing the major functions of the organization.

As you prepare to bring about change in an organization, remember that savvy entrepreneurial leaders are in tune with the fact that leaving a former way of doing business, or old procedures and practices, is an emotional period for employees which is likened to the death of what they know. To ease the pain of the change process, many organizations elect to hire a consultant to assist with major change intervention. Consultants will often use a strategy of conducting workshops with major constituents of the organization to obtain their input while at the same time breaking down resistance to change via open dialogue in the workshops. A word of caution about using a strategy of open dialogue and obtaining input: You can't ask for input and have open dialogue and then turn around and not utilize any suggestions made by employees. This can cause more internal morale problems than the change itself would cause.

The actual implementation of change is a very trying time for individuals and is a time filled with trials, tribulations, and a period of "getting the bugs out." An assessment of the change or changes made should occur to determine if the changes are appropriate, effective, and efficient. Then, the organization must be stabilized, with the change or changes becoming the new standard way of operating.

The diagram that follows illustrates the Organizational Change and depicts the importance of evaluating and diagnosing an environment in preparation for change while simultaneously preparing the organization for change and subsequently employing strategies to ease the pain of change acceptance and the birth of the new.

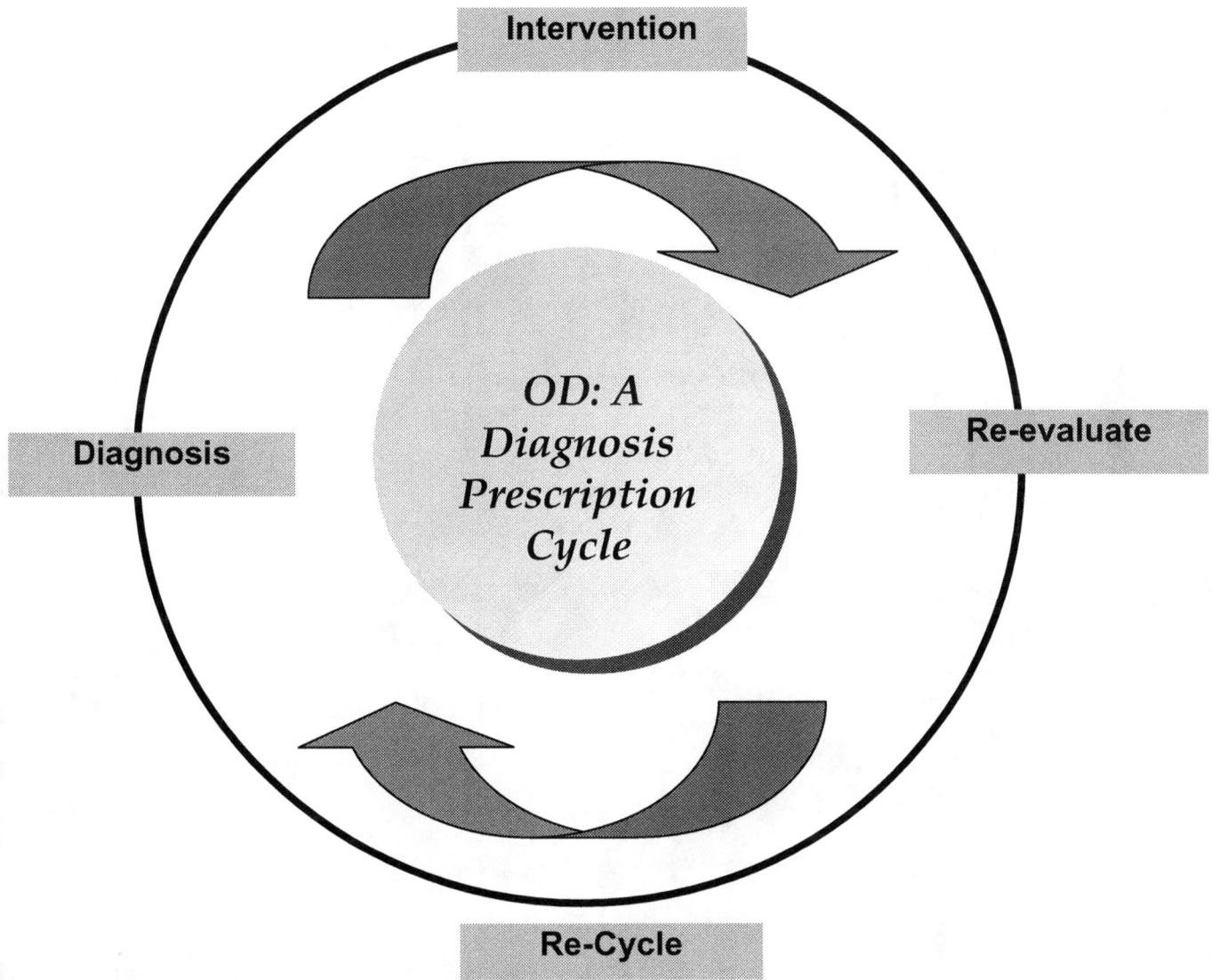

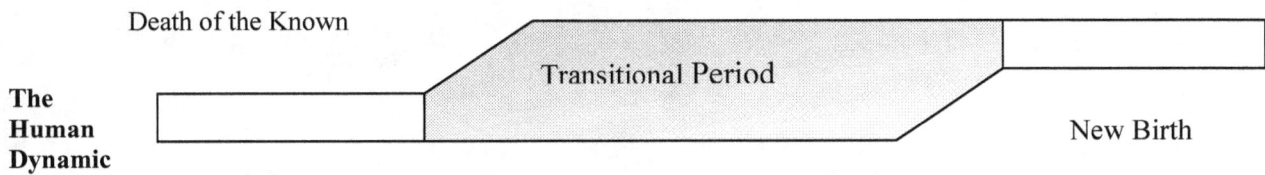

"Never give up on your dream

just because it's taking too long for it to become a reality.

The time will pass anyway,

so you might as well be working on realizing your dream. "

M.G.L.J.

Section IV

HITTING THE MARK:

21st CENTURY MARKETING

"The entrepreneurial leader is a walking and talking billboard

for her business.

You must present a professional appearance at all times,

even in the grocery store."

M.G.L.J.

Intercultural understanding and global astuteness are phrases becoming increasingly popular as well as recognized as key factors impacting the bottom line performance of progressive 21st Century businesses.

Companies of all types and sizes are entering the dynamic arena of international business. Venturing across borders and seas, however, is a step that requires in-depth research and much soul-searching. Not only does the entrepreneur need to know how to tell when the business is ready for the global market, but also must be aware of the challenges that await them when dealing in non-domestic regions.

The most significant challenge for small business owners deciding to enter into the international business arena will be the increased cost of doing business. International business is an expensive venture that requires a substantial investment of time, financial and human resources, and yes, patience and persistence.

We're talking here about time-consuming planning, including the investigation of financial, legal, production, and marketing issues. We're talking about time to become educated about international business, as well as learn cultures and perhaps even a foreign language. We're also talking about educating key staff members about the unique aspects of foreign markets, consumer behavioral patterns, politics, laws, and business practices.

Some major planning issues must, of course, be tackled, including which product to sell, needed product modifications for a global market, targeted countries, likely risks and obstacles, as well as the amount of company resources necessary and how the use of these resources will affect domestic operations. A good working knowledge of international trade rules, agreements, associations, and alliance is also a must.

Yes, there is an enormous amount of work and time involved in internationalizing operations, and internationalizing is certainly not right for all businesses. But, with the right match of products and services and a well-researched market base, the rewards can be great.

Whether you are growing the local or national market for your business or already exploring and pursuing international markets, you need to evaluate establishing your presence on the fastest growing marketing medium: The World Wide Web (WWW).

Why advertise on the WWW? The reasons are numerous. In addition to establishing your presence and enhancing your image in the market alongside your competition, the WWW allows your firm to reach a large mass market of educated consumers. The Web is available 24 hours a day, 7 days a week, year round. The results of Web advertising are immediately measurable interactively, customers incur no costs for obtaining information except the basic cost of having Internet connection, and your company materials can be updated or changed at any time.

You can get onto the fast lane of the "Information Super Highway" by creating a fully functional Web site. Successful marketing on the Web involves a multi-layered, interactive approach that keeps visitors interested. It should make visitors to your Web home feel involved and make them interested in touring your business. You can also have fill-in forms which enable you to collect data about visitors to your site as well as distribute documents or software by allowing them to download directly to their computers from your Web site. And certainly the inclusion of an e-mail address creates a link from your Web site to your office for addressing further reader inquiries. As you prepare your Web site, address the following questions: What am I selling? How can customers buy my products or services? Who am I? Why should someone buy what I am selling? Your Web site should provide answers to all of these questions.

You secure your Web site address by registering your domain or Web address. Many domain registration and Web site hosting services are available by searching the Internet. To connect to the Internet, you must pay for access through network access providers which can also be evaluated by searching the Internet. These providers offer a range of services and applications that can be tailored to your specific needs. There are many different types of Internet providers which include commercial online access providers such as America OnLine.

Ten years ago, a business with a Web site was unique; but now it is expected, especially among companies that wish to be thought of as technologically advanced and recognized for their business savvy. To maximize your use of the numerous technological advances in the area of computer marketing, you should contact a computer consultant who can assess the actual needs for your particular business and design your Web site for maximum benefit.

Promotion involves persuading the target market to purchase your product or service. Sales promotion can use either **direct** or **indirect** methods. **Direct** promotion methods include advertising, publicity, displays, special-event sales, and personal selling; whereas, **indirect** promotion methods include public relations, customer relations, customer services, and product packaging. An important part of promotion is advertising. For the new firm, advertising is particularly important because new or potential customers must be made aware of the firm's existence. Even though word-of-mouth advertising is fine and, in fact, crucial, a firm cannot rely solely on this form of advertising. Small business people need to incorporate advertising costs into their budgets, allocating monthly amounts in this area. To be successful, advertising must be consistent, image building, and continuous. The new entrepreneur needs to start off with advertising which will bring immediate action, called immediate response ads.

> *Your reputation is your most valuable asset; take all necessary measures to protect it at all times.*
> M.G.L.J.

There are a variety of advertising media which can be used.

- The Internet

- Newspapers

- Magazines

- Radio

- Direct Mail

- Television

- Point-of-Purchase Displays

- Bench Advertising

- Billboards

- Motion Advertising (public transportation)

- Fliers

- Speciality items or novelty items, such as pens, calendars, etc.

- Free publicity

- Telephone book

The selection of the best media for a small firm is not an easy endeavor. The Internet is a common advertising medium for the 21st Century, bringing your products and services to the world with the click of a mouse. Television is not appropriate for most small firms due to the cost factor and the probability that you may be reaching many individuals who are not in your target market, thus incurring unnecessary costs. Cable television advertising is generally a less expensive alternative. Large newspapers are another option, but they also tend to be quite expensive. Local or community papers may be a viable option, as they are less costly. Magazines are costly, and with the exception of local magazines, may cover too much territory for a small business unless regional inserts are available. Advertising spots on a local radio station may be feasible if the costs are in line and you can get the most advantageous time for reaching your target market.

Billboards tend to be effective near the location of the business but also are costly. Speciality advertisements, which include calendars, sweatshirts, and pens may be effective and can be as costly or as inexpensive as you desire. Motion advertising is effective if your market uses transportation such as buses, taxis, and subways on a routine basis. The telephone book should not be overlooked, as many potential customers do pre-shopping by the phone. Direct-mail advertising is used by a great number of small businesses. It is less expensive than many other forms of advertising and provides the small business owner with selective coverage.

The goal of advertising is to sell by way of the **AIDA** formula. This formula means you must get the potential customers' **<u>attention</u>,** make them **<u>interested</u>** in your product or service, create a **<u>desire</u>** for your product, and bring about **<u>action</u>,** the purchase of your product or service.

A succinct listing of basic advertising guidelines is summarized in the box which follows.

Basic Advertising Guidelines

1. Start with the sales budget.

   - Decide what percentage of your anticipated sales volume to allocate to advertising.

2. Profile yourself and your customers.

   - What business am I in?

   - What quality of merchandise do I sell?

   - What kind of image do I want to project?

   - How do I compare with the competition?

   - What customer services do I offer?

   - What are my customers' tastes?

   - Why will they buy from me?

3. Select advertising media.

4. Adhere to the following pointers for printed ads.

   - Make ads easy to recognize.

   - Use simple layouts.

   - Use dominant illustrations to feature merchandise.

   - Show the product's benefits to the reader.

   - Feature an item that is wanted, timely, adequately stocked, and typical of your store.

   - State a price or range of prices.

   - Include the store's name, address, telephone number, and Web site.

   - Repeat an ad if the response is good.

5. **AIDA**: Get the customer's **attention**, arouse their **interest**, make them **desire** your product, and finally, get them to take **action** to buy your product. This is the goal of advertising.

Brochures are an excellent way to communicate quickly and professionally the unique features of your business. Unfortunately, too many small business owners cut costs in the area of promotion and forget to develop this important promotional instrument which can effectively, simply, and relatively inexpensively, sell their business.

A dynamic brochure can cost many thousands of dollars to design and produce, or it can cost less than a hundred dollars. Needless to say, the less expensive model may not be as dynamic; but if designed and produced attractively and creatively with professional assistance, its impact can still be great.

If you are concerned with limiting costs, as most small business owners are, you first need to be aware of the common costs associated with developing a brochure and then determine how some of these costs can be cut.

Some Common Brochure Cost Considerations

▪ *Art Work*	▪ *Graphic Designer*
▪ *Layout*	▪ *Printing (Each ink color costs extra.)*
▪ *Photography*	▪ *Paper*
▪ *Paste Up*	▪ *Folding*
▪ *Illustration*	▪ *Die Cutting*
▪ *Typesetting*	▪ *Postage Permit for Bulk Mailing*
▪ *Brochure Design Consultant*	▪ *Postage Paid Permit*

To cut costs you may want to employ simple tactics such as limiting the brochure to one standard color (not one that has to be specially blended). If you want the effect of more than one color, check into the ways a printer can screen color for shade variations. Clip art taken from special graphic art books can be found at many libraries, by special mail order, and of course, on the computer. The use of clip art can cut the cost of paying for illustrations and artist fees, but make sure you have copyright permission to use the art.

"Good quality" paper in an attractive color with an effective layout can even make an appealing brochure using only black ink. On the topic of color, in selecting the color of paper or ink for your brochure, it is important to note that certain colors are said to provoke different reactions psychologically.

Psychology of Colors

Pink...Good Health

Yellow...Sunny, Cheery

Green...Nature, Harmony

Purple...Richness, Dignity

Blue...Coolness, Serenity

Red...Activity, Warmth

In addition to color, the brochure designer will be called upon to make decisions related to layout, format, and the flow of the brochure material, as well as typestyle of the print to be used. You may elect to design your brochure as a mailer with bulk rate postage; or you may also want a return mailer for recipients to request additional information, perhaps with pre-paid postage. Your decisions related to all of these considerations will depend on the particulars of your business, your market, your desires, and the cash position of your business.

Your finished brochure should be simple, attractive, eye appealing, clear, and easy to read and understand. It should be written in a manner that speaks to the reader and should convey key information about your business. The brochure should be action-producing (should entice people to purchase what you are offering) and believable.

Regardless of whether you decide to have a brochure that is elaborate or simple, brochures can be an effective tool to broach your market and capture sales.

A good public relations program can be the best way to maximize your advertising dollars. Public relations involves all activities that allow your business to be projected in a positive light and give your firm additional credibility.

A good public relations program should be multi-faceted in nature, incorporating varied activities, including public appearances on talk shows, public speaking, workshops, seminars, sponsorship of special events, and donations of time and/or materials to special causes. Even a great public relations program will not realize its full beneficial potential unless you communicate with the public. Press releases are the most common vehicle used to keep the media informed, and it is up to you to "toot our horn" with an interesting slant. The burden rests on you to inform the media about your activities in a useful and interesting fashion.

A good public relations program will submit something to the media, whether it is published or not, at least once a month.

What to publicize?

- *New employees or employee promotions*

- *New products or services*

- *Company anniversary*

- *Grand opening*

- *A new major client*

- *Speeches, workshops, seminars*

- *Charitable activities*

But how do I make news when nothing special is happening?

- *Use a prediction release to make predictions about industry and environmental trends.*

- *Consider a state-of-the-industry release that picks up on national industry information and discusses it from a local vantage point.*

- *Celebrity testimonial*

- *New or unusual usage of an existing product*

Public relations is crucial and is a viable, cost-effective way to enhance your firm's exposure and increase the profit line with minimal cost. Also, keep in mind that few businesses become very successful without giving back to the community in some way.

Sharing newsworthy information to the media about your business is an important key to free advertising for your business. The simplest activity or event could be newsworthy. It's up to you, however, to present the information to the media.

A press release format should be used to increase your chances for publicity as you make it easy for the media to evaluate the event and make a decision about coverage. Don't become disheartened if you send several releases and receive no coverage. Many, many factors go into the media's determining to give your event coverage. Sometimes the simple lack of availability of reporters at the time of your event, lack of newspaper space, uncommitted air time, deadlines or the timeliness of your press release can determine if you obtain exposure.

A few basic guidelines should be kept in mind when drafting a press release:

- *Select a subject for your press release with an angle that will entice the media to give you coverage.*

- *Details should be presented in short, clear sentences and paragraphs and, of course, free of typos and poor grammar.*

- *The press release should answer the questions of WHO, WHAT, WHEN, WHERE, and HOW.*

- *Make press releases short; one page is advisable.*

- *The press release should be computer generated and double spaced with one inch margins on all sides.*

- *Hand deliver or mail press releases first class to the targeted media. Include radio, TV, weekly and daily newspapers, trade publications, magazines, as well as wire services. Some media outlets prefer that press releases be submitted by e-mail, so contact your selected media to determine their preference.*

- *The press release should be received at least 24 hours before any event.*

- *Remember to include the contact person's name and phone number along with the release date.*

- *Capitalize on any and every opportunity to let the public hear about you and your business.*

A sample press release is provided for your convenient reference and appears below.

SAMPLE PRESS RELEASE

CATCHY HEADLINE

For Immediate Release
Date:
Contact Person:
Phone Number:

ACDC Enterprises has announced that Ms. Jane Smith has been appointed to Chairperson of the Board of Directors. The announcement was made by Mr. Jason Jones, CEO of ACDC Enterprises. *(You may include a date of announcement here.)*

Ms. Smith is currently serving as president of Johnson State University. *(Give Ms. Smith's professional background.*

Next, give a brief background of Ms. Smith's civic life. Ms. Smith is Chairperson of the Children's Relief Services, member of the Symphony Committee, a member of the Board of Directors of the Senior Citizens Fund Raising Organization, etc.

Then, briefly talk about the institution and include a statement from Mr. Jones as to the importance of this appointment.

Next, include some brief information on the company. ACDC enterprises is the second largest international culture consulting company in the southwest with over 2000 clients and 300 employees.

Finally, very briefly include personal data. Ms. Smith is married to Mr. Gerald Smith and they have two children.

A business card is a must for any business, no matter how large or small the endeavor. In addition to giving your business authenticity, a business card reflects your personal image and shows that you are serious about your business. A very effective, yet relatively inexpensive marketing tool, a business card acts as a billboard for your business, giving information and arousing interest in your business. Below are some important points to remember when designing your business card.

Always include the business name, address (P. O. Box or suite number), city, state, zip, phone number, fax number, pager, mobile phone, e-mail address, and Web address. If you are operating your business out of the home and don't want the public coming to your door, you may want to use a P. O. Box or suite number which many private postal services offer. Also make sure there is someone to answer your phone. Answering machines are generally a turn off, so consider using an answering service or voice message system when you're not available.

- You should include your name, a succinct descriptive line explaining what you do, and any appropriate affiliation or certifications that might give your business more credibility.

- A business logo or symbol continually associated with your business is important and should be incorporated into the business card design. Even if you use your name as your business name, be consistent with how it is imprinted; this will serve as your business logo. Also be consistent with the color scheme used.

- Use good quality card stock and select printing colors consistent with the color scheme you are using in your business.

- Try to be creative in your design; consider a Rolodex business card format if appropriate for the nature of your business.

Every call, incoming as well as outgoing, affords you an opportunity to sell your product, service, company, and professionalism. At the same time, every telephone contact your business has with the public can "unsell" your business and destroy credibility. Telemarketing is not just the worrisome folks who call selling something when you're enjoying the family dinner or just getting in from an exhausting day. Telemarketing also represents an effective, low-cost, high-yield marketing tactic for small firms.

Telemarketing, quite simply, is any marketing conducted by telephone designed to enhance your relationship with your customers, be they present customers, potential, or inactive customers. Telemarketing covers a whole range of activities from market surveys to customer service, account collections, and selling.

More specifically, telephone marketing techniques can be used as follows:

- *Identify New Markets*
- *Expand Market Share*
- *Generate, Screen and Qualify Leads*
- *Customer Service*
- *Reactivate Inactive Markets*
- *Collect Outstanding Debts*

- *Close Sales, Get New Orders, and Upgrade*
- *Conduct Surveys to Gather Information*
- *Complement Direct-Mail and TV Campaigns*
- *Turn One-Time Customers into Regular Clients*
- *Overcome Initial Customer Resistance*

Make all of your telephone contacts productive, professional, and profitable. Implement a comprehensive telemarketing plan utilizing sound marketing principles, telecommunications technology, and (effective and efficient) management techniques. You've already invested in a telephone so make this investment work for you!!!

Many entrepreneurs are attracted to the lure of making "a mint" by having an exhibit and selling to a large captive audience. While many exhibiters may not make "a mint," this can happen, but only if you really do your homework. You first need to be in tune with your purpose and objectives for displaying. Are you interested in an exhibit to make fast money or to simply obtain exposure for your business and make contacts. With your objectives in mind, you next need to investigate the nature of the convention attendees, numbers projected to be in attendance, and their mind-set when attending such a convention. For example, some professional associations will have an audience primarily desirous of simply looking at new products and services in their field, while other conventions have attendees who are looking for new and different items to buy ranging from computers to clothes. And, even though a convention is being held by a male organization, you may find that the norm is for wives to also attend who may be the main visitors to the exhibit hall with a buying mind-set.

The purpose of any exhibit-type show is to provide an environment for personal selling where total communication about your business products and services can be obtained with an identified target group. Such a situation can provide immediate sales or provide an excellent environment for qualifying large numbers of prospects. It also provides a chance to showcase your products and services while receiving marketing research data as to the appropriateness of your product or service for your identified target market.

To truly capitalize on the opportunities afforded by an exhibit show, the exhibitor needs to have a strategic show plan. Strategic show planning should include plans for a creative, enticing, professional display to include promotional materials, novelty items, and perhaps even a drawing which allows you to get business cards and information from booth visitors.

83

Plans should also include booth management training for personnel. Training should include strategies for meeting, qualifying, and targeting solid contacts; communicating succinctly what your firm is about; and tactics to obtain appropriate information to follow up on prospects. Certainly, if you plan to actually sell items at the convention or show, you will have to make many decisions pertaining to displaying your inventory. Considerations here include the amount of inventory to be displayed, shipping of your inventory to and from the show, and basic concerns pertaining to the actual sale of your items including the acceptance of credit cards, packaging, etc.

In today's competitive selling environment, astute entrepreneurs will certainly want to consider convention and trade show marketing as a way to expand their market. With the utilization of highly motivated and trained staff people coupled with a sound strategic plan, marketing via trade shows and conventions has enormous potential to increase your bottom line.

You produce or purchase what you believe to be best seller items that need to be marketed. You find that it is not feasible to have an establishment for selling these items and you can't find wholesalers or retailers willing to invest money in stocking your items in inventory. Now what do you do?

One option to get your merchandise exposed is through the use of consignment selling. Consignment selling in essence is a situation whereby goods are provided to a dealer who, in turn, pays you for the merchandise only when it sells, with the dealer keeping an agreed-upon percentage of the selling price.

Proposing such an arrangement certainly provides incentive for a dealer to carry your merchandise, as no monetary outlay is required on the dealer's part, and they are able to increase their merchandise offerings and potential profit areas. For the seller, such an arrangement provides for merchandise exposure to potential buyers and a chance to make money while limiting overhead costs.

This is a particularly appropriate strategy to use when your product has no track record to support a wholesaler's or retailer's carrying your merchandise when you know your product will sell. Consignment selling, thus, lets you get your "foot in the door" with desirable distributors.

Consignment selling does, however, have its disadvantages. You will receive no money until your merchandise sells; the merchandise is out of your control, so damage, loss, and shopper abuse may occur. You cannot control the shelving of your merchandise and since the consignee probably stands to make less money on your product versus his or her purchased inventory which he or she is motivated to sell because of the investment, maximum-exposure placement is hard to obtain.

Therefore, it is obvious that the consignee must be provided with an attractive incentive package. Where personal selling and knowledge of your product is important, the consignment arrangement benefits may again be minimized.

The relationship existing between you, the consignor, and the seller (consignee), should be clarified in writing. In selling items on consignment, it is best to have an attorney provide guidance in designing an appropriate, contract. Responsibility for loss or damage of merchandise, display of merchandise, commission arrangements, the length of time the merchandise will be placed on consignment, method and date of payment, return policy, selling price, etc. should all be addressed in a contractual agreement.

Consignment selling is not for everyone, but it is an inexpensive way to test market a product or to obtain product exposure, or even to sell to a non-traditional market.

One of the keys to a successful, thriving business is customer service. All too often the excited and struggling entrepreneur is so concerned about marketing, obtaining customers, and making ends meet that a simple ingredient such as customer service is overlooked. The bottom line is that consumers patronize businesses where they enjoy good customer treatment along with a quality product and service at an acceptable cost.

Of course, small business owners can ensure good service by knowing their clients' needs and extending courteous and efficient service. But this must be coupled with paying attention to details and the little things that give customers a "warm and fuzzy" feeling. This keeps them coming back and telling others about you. Additionally, listening to the desires of consumers, keeping promises, and meeting deadlines help build a reputation that creates consumer loyalty.

Research indicates that even though businesses know the importance of customer service, many still do not satisfy expectations, forgetting little things like "thank you" or a simple apology. Many small businesses have launched programs incorporating what is called a "Customer Satisfaction Measurement" (CSM). This is a method companies have developed in an effort to combat poor customer service. This technique can assist business owners in prioritizing problems and allocating resources to proper areas. Be it a simple survey, customer comment card, or simply observant and sensitized employees, CSM calls upon the business to keep records of complaints and to look upon complaints and suggestions as areas where perhaps some organizational change is necessary.

All small businesses should form their own process to capture complaints, handle problems, and garner suggestions along with developing creative ways to show customers that they value their business. The implementation of the process will require the training of employees to be in tune with the importance of the customer and to be empathetic. Any such process will also require the complete commitment of all employees along with a strong, structured monitoring and response system.

Don't forget to pay attention to details and to go the extra mile. Design a process to keep up with your customers, including their names, addresses, e-mail addresses, and maybe even birthdays. An unexpected card or novelty item can go a long way in making customers feel good about your business.

Section V

FINANCIAL SAVVY !!!!

"Never avoid the numbers.

They are the thermometer indicating the health

and wealth of your business."

M.G.L.J.

The financially savvy entrepreneurial leader needs to know the financial status of the business at all times, even if an accounting service is used. The following guideposts are provided to help the entrepreneur stay on top of the financial side of the business.

The entrepreneurial leader should

On a daily basis:

- *Know the amount of cash on hand.*

- *Know the bank balance.*

- *Know the daily summary of sales and cash receipts.*

- *Make sure that all errors in recording collections on accounts are corrected.*

- *Make sure that a record of all monies paid out, by cash or check, is maintained.*

On a weekly basis:

- *Check accounts receivable and take action on delinquent accounts.*

- *Check accounts payable and take advantage of discounts for early payment.*

- *Make sure payroll records are in order.*

- *Make sure taxes and reports to State and Federal Governments are prepared and sent.*

On a monthly basis:

- *Make sure that all Journal entries are posted to the General Ledger.*

- *Assess the Profit/Loss Statement.*

- *Assess the Balance Sheet.*

- *Make sure the Bank Statement is reconciled.*

- *Make sure the Petty Cash Account is in balance.*

- *Make sure that all Federal Tax Deposits, Withheld Income, FICA Taxes, and State Taxes are made.*

- *Make sure that Accounts Receivable are aged, i.e., 30, 60, 90 days, etc., and past-due accounts collected.*

- *Check inventory.*

So you have the vision. Your strategic plan has been formulated, and you're committed to making your business a success. You've grown your business to a point where you now need cash to expand to new horizons. Or, it may even seem that you need cash to simply get off of go or to sustain the present plateau, and the question now is: Where do I go to get money to fulfill the vision?

On the traditional side, the most common sources of funds include personal cash and savings, family, friends, business associates, equipment dealers, savings and loan companies, consumer and commercial finance companies, lines of credit, life insurance, small business investment companies, the federal government, venture capital firms, commercial banks, credit cards, mortgaging real estate, trade credit, suppliers, and selling ownership of the business.

Creative money hunt strategies are limited only to one's self-imposed box of thinking and can range from co-partnering and new empowerment zoning to collaborative relationships with non-profits. Gaining in popularity are angel networks which link successful businesspersons looking for investment opportunities with young, growing businesses. Also, many entrepreneurs are turning to factoring, new SBA funding programs, as well as money mentors for financial support.

There is not a prescribed, single best way to obtain money for your business. Each situation is unique, and you will need to evaluate thoroughly the options and determine a course appropriate for your needs.

The capital you need to be acquiring is often grouped into several categories:

1. **Fixed capital:** money for the building, equipment, fixtures, and vehicles.

2. **Working capital:** money for running the business on a day-to-day basis. This covers items such as utilities, money for buying inventory, insurance, advertising, salaries, rent, savings, cash, accounts receivable, etc.

3. **Funds for personal living costs (if you are a business owner):** capital to provide for you and your family until the business brings a profit.

4. **Money cushion:** extra money for unforeseen and unexpected costs.

It is crucial to have sufficient capital. The drawbacks of not having enough capital include:

- business failure

- inability to afford good employees

- investment in sub-standard or inadequate equipment

- inadequate inventory

- inability to obtain a good credit rating

- inability to obtain quantity discounts and other cost advantages

After thoroughly assessing your monetary requirements for starting and operating your venture, you will need to identify sources from which monies can be obtained for starting and operating your venture. There are many ways to obtain money to start and operate your business. Business financing is categorized as either **equity** or **debt financing**.

Equity financing represents money which the owner and/or others put into the business. All parties are at risk and at the same time stand to reap rewards. Equity financing is used for starting a business, expanding a business, and financing acquisitions. Equity financing includes personal savings and assets, money from family and friends, investments by key employees, and funds from venture capitalists.

Debt financing, on the other hand, is money loaned to businesses for a fee or interest. The funds borrowed, therefore, must be repaid. Debt financing is also used for business start up, operating funds, and expansion funds. Debt financing includes funds from commercial banks, savings and loans, savings bonds, commercial finance companies, small business investment corporations, federal programs, franchisers, or project organizers.

There are many sources from which funds may be borrowed. They include the following:

Private Investors. Members of the family, friends, business associates, equipment dealers (if the equipment is bought on an installment basis or leased), and wholesalers of products (when they offer 30 to 90 days of credit before demanding payment).

Business Firms. Various business sources, such as:

- Banks

- Savings and loan companies which refinance home mortgages and make property improvement loans

- Personal finance companies

- Finance companies which provide commercial credit (listed in the yellow pages and advertised in classified and financial sections of newspapers)

- Life insurance companies (some make loans to policy holders)

- Small business investment companies (these companies are licensed by the Small Business Administration to make long-term loans and guarantee bank loans, and they will provide equity financing by actually buying a share of the business)

- Development corporations which are formed by private citizens or businesses to promote the economy in their area

- Venture capital associations or groups of investors looking for businesses with promising futures (they usually provide equity financing, and they often advertise in the classified section of the newspaper Want Ads and via various Web site listings)

Federal Government. Some of the federal funding sources available are:

- Small Business Administration (SBA)

- Veterans Administration (VA)

Commercial Banks. One of the major sources of borrowing capital is a local commercial bank. It is crucial to have good rapport with your banker. Loans are generally either short-term or long-term in nature. Short-term generally represents money extended for a year or less, and long-term represents money extended for a period longer than a year. Loans are categorized as **secured/collateral** loans or **unsecured**. In the first type, the borrower is asked to pledge something such as life insurance, securities, equipment, real estate, or some other asset belonging to the loan seeker or the business. In the second instance, no security is required; and the loan is made based more on one's financial reputation, managerial ability, bank's evaluation of the business's soundness, etc. Your personal character, business reputation, adequate records, ability to repay the loan, and suitable collateral are all important necessities in obtaining a loan.

Personal Savings, Family and Friends. Your personal savings should be used as a last resort. If you obtain a loan from a bank, always spend the bank's money first.

Friends and family will frequently be receptive to lending you money, particularly if your business plan reflects significant research, and you can convince them that you can give them a greater return on their money than they would be able to obtain from a bank. Be sure when using this form of financing that you protect yourself with a buy-back contract or promissory note at the beginning of the financial relationship. The contract should make it worthwhile for your friends and family to invest in your business. At the same time, it should protect your ownership in the company when you become highly successful. Be cautious with family and friends' financial assistance. Personal relationships can become extremely strained when money is involved.

Life Insurance Policies. Individuals can borrow a major percentage of the cash value of their life insurance policies that have "paid-in" equity. These loan rates are generally much lower than bank loan rates. This form of financing should be investigated if you have such policies, but make sure you know any and all ramifications of borrowing on the equity.

Credit Cards. Credit cards are the most expensive way to finance your business due to the comparatively high interest rates. Try to avoid this form of financing.

Suppliers. Be familiar with all trade credit options. Creative terms with vendors can significantly affect your cash flow so that you have more money available when it is needed. Also, many suppliers, just for the asking, will pay you money if you are using their products. For example, a manufacturer or distributor of play gyms may compensate you if you advertise that you are only using their specially constructed and safe equipment.

Real Estate Mortgages. Mortgages on residential property may sometimes be used to finance a business. You should contact your mortgage company for specific information about this form of financing. Be sure to assess the ramifications of using this form of financing, including the fact that you may lose your property if the loan is not repaid in a timely manner.

Savings and Loan Associations. Savings and loan associations historically have specialized in real estate financing, making loans on commercial, industrial, and residential properties. Savings and loan associations are now also beginning to offer the usual type of business loans available through commercial banks.

Venture Capitalists. Venture capitalists are affluent investors who need tax write-offs. They will invest money in your firm in return for your making them limited partners in your business. The majority of all new businesses have losses at first, and some wealthy investors are looking for losses to get tax breaks. You should obtain the assistance of an accountant and attorney before getting involved with venture capitalists.

Small Business Administration. The SBA defines a small business as a profit-making entity that is independently owned and operated and not dominant in its field. They have the specific objective of promoting the small business contribution to the nation's economic growth. By law, they are not allowed to make a loan if the funds can be obtained from a bank or other private source. Therefore, the first step is to try to obtain financing through regular channels. If the loan is turned down, then ask the bank to make the loan under SBA's Loan Guaranty Plan or participate with SBA in a loan. If the banker is interested, ask her or him to contact the SBA to discuss your application. Usually the SBA will deal directly with the banker. The Small Business Administration will consider making a direct loan when these other forms of financing are not obtainable.

Some of the of types of loans available from SBA include the following:

1. Guarantee Loan: The SBA will guarantee up to a certain amount of money loaned to a small businessperson.

2. Participation Loan: SBA and the lending institution each put up part of the funds for the loan.

3. Economic Opportunity Loan: The SBA will lend money to any resident of the United States, Puerto Rico, or Guam if:

   a. Total family income from all sources (excluding welfare) is not sufficient for the basic needs of the family, and

   b. Due to social or economic disadvantages, the person has been denied the opportunity to acquire adequate financing through normal channels or reasonable terms. This includes honorably discharged Vietnam-era veterans.

4. Lease Guarantee Program: This is the issuance of an insurance policy or the reinsuring of a policy issued by a private insurance company which guarantees the rent for a small businessperson. A small business is often unable to lease a strategic location because it does not have a prime credit rating as required by some property owners. A guarantee that the rent default will not occur is a valuable negotiating tool in locating a site.

5. Minority Loans: Loans are processed under somewhat relaxed criteria to encourage minority individuals to pursue business ownership.

The SBA also furnishes individual assistance to small businesspersons in the form of counseling, advice, and specific information about various types of business enterprises. The SBA requires all information and an assortment of papers that any other lender would. They will ask the same questions. They require collateral or some other guarantee of repayment, though good character and business ability may weigh more heavily with them than with a bank. However, they do state that the borrower should be able to provide sufficient funds from his or her own resources to have a reasonable amount at stake in the early stages of a new business. Certain SBA loan programs are phased in and others eliminated periodically, so check with your local SBA office for additional information.

Veterans Administration. The purpose of the VA program is to enable the veteran to obtain home, farm or business real estate, supplies and equipment, and working capital. The VA guarantees or insures various types of loans made by private lenders. If you qualify, then the various lenders (banks, savings and loans, etc.) would have to be contacted to determine if they make VA business loans and to set up an appointment. If a loan is not available in this way, the VA can make a direct loan in some cases.

Additional Ways of Obtaining Financing. Various other types of financing are as follows:

1. Financing by selling ownership of the business: Partnership arrangements, corporate arrangements, and public venture capitalists, or small business investment companies (SBICs) which are privately owned venture capital firms eligible for federal loans to invest in or lend to businesses.

2. Commercial Finance Companies: Firms which specialize in higher risk loans and generally charge higher interest rates than commercial banks.

3. Consumer Finance Companies: Financing arranged as a personal loan to one or several of the people in the business.

4. Trade Credit: Obtaining credit and financing from suppliers by their extension of terms of payment.

5. Factoring: This form of financing involves the outright sale of a business' accounts receivable to another firm, called a factor. The factor then pays cash to the business for its accounts receivable at a charge for each invoice plus interest on its advance.

Pointers for Successful Debt Financing

✓ If you are presently working, try to borrow funds while still employed. Studies show that banks are less likely to give you a loan when you do not have a "steady" job.

✓ Make sure that you have devoted great attention to your marketing plan. Bankers want to know that there is actually a substantial market for your business and that you know how to capture the market successfully.

✓ Be able to sell yourself to the banker, and this includes looking like a businessperson.

✓ Try to search out a banker who is familiar with your industry.

✓ Fill out loan documents and applications neatly and accurately.

✓ Keep trade secrets to yourself. Do not share the details of your unique features unnecessarily. Share enough to establish the fact that you can obtain the competitive edge in the market, but the banker does not need to know everything.

✓ Under capitalization is a major cause of business failure. Make sure you have accurately assessed your start-up and working capital requirements for at least one year before you initiate your venture. Examine all of the financing sources mentioned in this chapter and determine what is right for you. A sample personal financial statement is included in the appendix to help you determine your personal net worth and assess what collateral you may have to assist you in finding funds for your venture.

Prior to approaching a lending institution or investors for assistance in funding your business, you will need to make sure you have the answers to the following questions.

Monetary Considerations

- How much money do you need?

- What exactly do you need the money for? Some specific reasons for needing money include buying inventory, equipment, supplies, renting space, salaries, money to meet financial obligations to suppliers, etc.

- What collateral do you have? What do you or your business own which can be offered as security for money received?

- When do you need the money?

- How long do you need the money?

- Can you afford the cost of the money?

- Where can you find the money? Make sure you have backups in place.

REMEMBER, IT IS BETTER TO OVERESTIMATE THAN UNDERESTIMATE YOUR FINANCIAL REQUIREMENTS!!

The novice entrepreneurial leader probably would want to use the services of an accountant to set up the appropriate business accounting records. The following information is designed to provide some insight into the types of records the accountant should establish, the purpose of each of these records, and the information they should provide.

Before obtaining funds from whichever source is feasible, it is necessary to have accurate financial records and statements to present to the potential funder. These records are also necessary for successful business operations. Keeping accurate, concise, and appropriate business records is necessary for business success. A great majority of businesses that have failed did not keep accurate records. Good records show whether a business is making a profit, how much profit, and whether the business is efficient and growing. Good records also help you to identify specific problem areas.

For the purpose of efficient business operations as well as funding attainment, all businesses need the following basic financial records:

Basic Financial Records

- A Record of Cash and Record of Sales Receipts

- Accounts Payable Record

- Accounts Receivable Record

- The Balance Sheet

- Cash Payments Journal

- Payroll Record

- Schedule of Depreciation

- Withdrawal and Capital Record

Good records should show the financial status of the business, trends in the business, and provide important information about the business as well as point to problem areas.

Although financial records often seem overwhelming, the small business owner doesn't have to be an accountant to keep good records and understand the financial statements generated from those records. The basic records are described below.

Accounts Payable Record represents a list of one's suppliers and the amount owed to each.

Accounts Receivable Record shows a list of what each credit customer owes you. It should also show what and when each customer purchases, and is a record of all payments received.

The Balance Sheet lists the firm's assets and liabilities. A statement of the firm's current position, the Balance Sheet shows where the business stands at the end of an accounting period. It shows what the business is worth, what the owner owes, and its obligations. To be accurate, total assets must equal total liabilities plus owner's equity.

Cash Payments Journal shows all expenditures, including date and reason.

The Income Statement, or sometimes called the Profit/Loss Statement, lists the total sales, cost of goods sold, expenses, and taxes required in order to obtain a profit, usually for a period of a month. It may take different forms, but is generally a statement of the total amount of goods or services sold less all expenses and costs levied against sales to determine profit or loss from one's operations.

Payroll Record shows gross and new amounts of salaries paid, date of transactions, amount of taxes withheld, and holdings.

Schedule of Depreciation calculates the decrease in value of equipment and furnishings so as to determine net worth. Depreciation schedules are basically lists of the major equipment and furnishings a company owns.

Withdrawal and Capital Record shows what the owner puts in or takes out of the business and stands as a record of transactions which affect ownership.

Sales forecasting requires you to predict the future as accurately as possible with justification for the forecasted figures. A forecast can be based on past sales trends, interviews with people operating similar businesses, various types of published data, information from experts, market calculations, as well as your personal judgement. Factors to take into consideration when forecasting sales include the forecasts for individual product lines which can often be obtained from your suppliers' industry trends for your area; forecasts of your state's gross national product for your city, county, area, and industry; unique characteristics of your area, and an assessment of your competition.

One approach to developing a sales forecast begins by estimating the total number of persons in the selected target market. This estimate comes from an analysis of your market via a survey and also from secondary sources such as Statistical Abstracts of the U. S., marketing and demographic informational sources, and industry publications.

The following four equations will allow you to forecast sales:

> *(1) T x A = TPM*
>
> *(2) TPM x P = TAM*
>
> *(3) TAM x EMS = SIU*
>
> *(4) SIU x PR = SID*

Explanation:

(1) T x A = TPM

Total number of people in the target market multiplied by the **annual** number of purchases per person = **total potential market.**

106

(2) TPM x P = TAM

Total potential market multiplied by the **percent** of the total market coverage you think you might be able to obtain = **total available market**.

(3) TAM x EMS = SIU

Total available market multiplied by the **expected market share** you expect to obtain = **sales forecast in units**.

(4) SIU x PR = SID

Sales forecast in units multiplied by the **price per unit** = **sales forecast in dollars**.

When determining your expected market share, be sure to take into consideration the present market share of your competitors, the amount of promotion you will be using compared to your competition, the sales trends of similar products, and what the present competition may do to improve their present product or service when you enter the market.

A number of ratios can be drawn from the Balance Sheet and utilized as management tools. Three of the most common ratios are the liquidity ratios: **working capital**, **current ratio,** and **acid test ratio**. Each ratio has general standards that are considered acceptable, but to be most effective the ratios must be compared to industry standards.

WORKING CAPITAL = Current Assets - Current Liabilities

This ratio is of interest to short-term creditors, as it shows how well the firm will be able to pay its creditors when due.

CURRENT RATIO = Current Assets divided by Current Liabilities

Shows, in general terms, how well the business can cover its current bills. The general rule of acceptability is 2 to 1.

ACID-TEST = (Current Assets - Inventory) divided by Current Liabilities

Measures how well a company can meet its obligations without having to liquidate inventory. A ratio of 1 to 1 is adequate.

Accounts Receivable are a very crucial component of the current assets of a business, as they basically represent a firm's money being used by others. Extending credit can bolster a company's sales and at the same time suffocate the business. No sale is ever completed until the money is collected. Credit management requires the use of credit applications that include an explanation of collection procedures. The business owner ultimately decides who will receive credit and how much they will receive. It is important to maintain tight collection procedures, as most retail customers are unlikely to pay bills more than 90 days old. When a bill becomes more than 40 days past due, the business has a collection problem.

Make sure an invoice is included or mailed on the day the product or service is delivered. The invoice should be clear, easy to understand, and include information concerning terms and assessments for late payment. Send reminders to the customer if the payment is not received when due, and again at the end of 15 and 30 days past due. At 40 days past due or before, telephone the customer and get a definite commitment for the method, time, and amount of payment. Record this information and call again at 55 days past due if no action has been taken on the part of the customer. At 70 days past due, visit the customer, determined to collect some form of payment. Collections agencies are expensive; use them only as a last resort or if you have a large number of outstanding accounts.

Consider front-end handling charges for those customers who are consistently past due. Although it may seem as a gesture of goodwill to put off collection for some customers, it is much better to set up a partial payment schedule that may allow the customer extra time for total payment than to ignore business collection procedures altogether. If a check bounces, call the customer immediately. Bad check charges can cost a company dearly. Weigh the customer's business against their overall cost to the business in determining if it would be more advantageous to put them on a cash only basis or drop their business entirely. Balance customer service and courtesy with firm collection strategies. Above all, remember that persistence in the use of collection procedures is the key to effective credit management.

Beginning on the next page, a standard financial vocabulary is given in convenient reference format.

Angels	People who may be willing to supply capital to an entrepreneur with no strings attached. These individuals may include relatives, friends, or a mentor.
Asset	*An item of value owned by a business or individual.*
Balance Sheet	*A financial statement which lists the firm's assets and liabilities. It shows what the business is worth.*
Balloon Payment	A final payment generally on an installment loan that is larger than the preceding payment.
Bankrupt	The state of a person or firm unable to pay creditors and judged legally insolvent.
Bond	A long-term instrument used to finance the capital needs of a business or government unit.
Break-Even Point	The volume of sales at which the firm's costs equal its income. Above the break-even point, a firm is making money. Below the break-even point, a firm is losing money.
Budget	An itemized summary of probable expenditures and income for a given period of time with a plan for meeting expenses.
Capital	Cash or cash equivalents necessary to fund a business entity
Capital Asset	An asset with a life of more than one year that is not bought and sold in the ordinary course of business activity.
Capital Budgeting	The process of planning expenditures on assets whose returns are expected to extend beyond one year.
Capital Gain/Losses	Profits (or losses) on the sale of capital assets owned for six months or more.
Cash Flow	A financial projection utilized by business owners to evaluate receipts and disbursements over time. A cash forecast in used to predict high and low points in regard to profitability.

111

Cash Management	The practice of using the firm's money to earn money rather than allowing it to remain in accounts which do not pay interest.
Collateral	Property, stocks, bonds, savings accounts, life insurance, and current business assets which may be held to insure repayment of a loan.
Commercial Bank	An ordinary bank of deposit and discount, with checking accounts, as distinguished from a savings bank.
Contingency Fund	Monies set aside for unexpected expenditures.
Cost-Benefit Analysis	An analytic technique of weighing the costs of a project or investment against the benefits derived therefrom.
Debt Capital	Monies loaned to the business owner which are used to increase and enhance the value of the firm. The money plus interest must be repaid over time and represents a debt for the firm.
Debt Financing	Debt incurred when the business firm borrows funds for certain business purposes
Disposable Income	Personal income remaining after the deduction of taxes on personal income and other compulsory payments.
Dun & Bradstreet	A mercantile agency which offers credit ratings, financial analysis, and other financial services, usually on a contractual basis.
EBIT	Abbreviation for earnings before interests and taxes.
Equity	The net worth of a business which consists of capital stocks, capital (or paid) surplus, earned surplus (or retained earnings), and sometimes, certain net worth reserves.
Equity Capital	Money obtained by selling a part of the interest in the business.
Fixed Assets	Assets of a business which are relatively permanent and are necessary for the functioning of the firm. Fixed assets include buildings, furniture, equipment, etc.
Goodwill	Intangible asset based on the good image of a firm and established by the excess of the price paid for the going concern over its book value.

Gross Income	Amount received by the firm before deducting operating expenses.
Investment Prospectus	A document which highlights the major information regarding a business. This document summarizes information so that potential investors can quickly and easily evaluate a business venture.
Investment Tax Credit	A credit from federal income taxes that is computed as a percentage of the initial cost of certain capital assets.
Line of Credit	An arrangement whereby a financial institution commits itself to lend a firm or individual up to a specified maximum amount of funds during a specified period.
Liquidation	The process of terminating a firm's existence by selling its assets and paying its debts.
Liquidity	A firm's cash position and its ability to meet maturing obligations.
Net Profit	The amount earned by the firm after paying expenses and taxes.
Net Worth	The difference between assets and liabilities.
Operating Expenses	General expenses incurred by the business to generate sales.
Overhead	All of the costs of a business other than direct labor and materials.
Owner's Equity	The amount of cash or other assets the owner has invested in the business.
Payback Period	The length of time required for the net revenues of an investment to equal the cost of the investment.
Price/Earnings Ratio	The ratio of price per share to earnings per share.
Profit-Loss Statement	Also called the Income Statement, this financial statement lists the total sales, cost of goods sold, expenses, and taxes required in order to obtain a profit, usually for a period of a month.
Trade Credit	Inter-firm debt arising through credit sales and recorded as an account receivable by the seller and as an account payable by the buyer.

Under-Capitalization	The lack of necessary funds to optimally start and operate a venture.
Venture Capital	Cash or cash equivalents supplied by an outside party who specializes in providing working capital for small and/or growing businesses. Venture capitalists require an equity interest in the firm in return for supplying capital assistance.
Working Capital	Current assets minus current liabilities.

Section VI

"LEGAL EZE"

"It's not the one who falls that fails,

but the one who falls, gives up, and never gets up."

M.G.L.J.

There are a variety of legal forms of business ownership. One form cannot be said to be better than the other, as one must consider the advantages and disadvantages of each in light of the nature of the business and the desires of the business owner. Below, the common forms are presented in terms of their advantages and disadvantages.

Proprietorship

An enterprise owned by one individual is a **proprietorship**. The owner and the business are one and the same and cannot be legally distinguished and separated in the eyes of the law. This is the most common form of legal ownership.

Advantages

- It is fairly easy to start.

- Legal assistance is not a necessity.

- The organizational structure is simple.

- The owner has freedom to make decisions and enjoy the profits.

- It is easy to dissolve.

Disadvantages

- The owner is liable for all the enterprise's debts.

- Liability is not limited to the amount of capital/total assets invested in the business. The owner's home, car, bank account, and other possessions may be claimed by people to whom he or she owes money.

117

- If the owner has personal debts, creditors can take assets of the business to satisfy demands.

- Sometimes it is difficult to obtain funding.

- Success is dependent on the owner's abilities.

- The legal life of the business terminates with the death of the owner.

Partnership

A **partnership** is the joining of two or more individuals to form an organization.

Advantages

- Gives you the opportunity to pool financial resources.

- Provides the advantages of combining the additional skills and knowledge of partners. Allows the teaming of individuals who have complementary talent.

- Allows for division of labor and management responsibility.

Disadvantages

- General partners have unlimited liability.

- The death of a partner terminates the partnership.

- General partners are responsible for the acts of each other partner.

- Partners cannot obtain bonding protection against the acts of other partners.

- There is the possibility of disagreement among partners.

There are two different types of partnerships:

1) **General** - Each partner is held liable for the acts of other partners.

2) **Limited** - This form can only be created by compliance with a state's statutory requirements. It is composed of one or more general partners. The liability of the limited partner is restricted to the amount he or she contributes.

A partnership should have an attorney draw up a partnership agreement. The partnership agreement usually includes sections addressing the following:

- name, purpose, and location

- duration of agreement

- type of partnership

- contribution by partners

- business expansion (how it will be handled)

- authority

- books, records, and the method of accounting

- division of profits and losses

- salaries

- rights of continuing partnership

- death of partner

- employee negotiations

- release of debts

- sale of partnership interests

- arbitration

- addition, alterations, and/or modification of partnership agreement

- settlement of disputes

- required and prohibited acts

- absence and disability

Corporation

A **corporation** is a legal entity which is separate and distinct from the individual. In the new or very small corporation, the stock in the corporation is described as "closed" or "closely held" and is not available to the general public in order for the owners to keep control.

Advantages

- The corporate form of ownership offers permanence--the business does not cease to exist if an owner dies.

- Owners of a corporation have limited liability (only the amount invested in the business).

- Corporations usually have greater borrowing power.

- Transferring ownership is relatively easy.

- The corporate federal income tax rates are below the tax brackets for individuals

- Company expansion is relatively easy.

- In figuring the corporation's net income, salaries paid to employees and executives may be deducted as an expense item.

Disadvantages

- Incorporations can be expensive and require detailed records which are often costly and time consuming.

- Corporate income is taxed twice. First, the corporation pays tax on its income before it distributes dividends, and then shareholders pay taxes on dividends.

- The powers of the corporation are limited to those stated in the charter.

- The corporate form of ownership is more impersonal than the other forms.

S Corporations

The **S Corporation**, formerly known as the Subchapter S Corporation, is a form of organization which is specifically designed for closely held firms. The major difference between this type of corporation and regular corporations is the way in which they are taxed. In S Corporations, the profits are distributed to shareholders according to how much stock they own. The shareholders pay tax on the profits as personal income, with the corporation paying no tax as an entity. In essence, the stockholders are taxed as partners, thus avoiding the corporate income tax structure while allowing the firm to retain the limited liability feature of corporations.

S Corporations have many legal restrictions, including limitations to the number of stockholders, who may be stockholders, how profits are distributed, and the amount of fringe benefits allowed owner/employees.

You should consult your attorney and accountant to determine the advantages and disadvantages of this and other forms of ownership for your particular business. You should also consult your accountant about all tax considerations prior to actually implementing your business.

Limited Liability Company

The **Limited Liability Company (LLC)** is a hybrid between a partnership and a corporation in that it combines the "pass-through" treatment of a partnership with the limited liability accorded to corporate shareholders.

Advantages

- Historically, most states require that a Limited Liability Company (LLC) be comprised of at least two LLC members. Today, most states and the IRS recognize the single-member LLC as a legitimate business structure.

- Like limited partnerships and corporations, the Limited Liability Company shares a similar advantage--it is recognized as a separate legal entity from its "members."

- Most states require that fewer formalities be observed in an LLC in comparison to a corporation.

- The LLC owner's liability is generally limited to the amount of money which the person has invested in the LLC. Thus, LLC members are offered the same limited liability protection as a corporation's shareholders.

- LLCs allow for pass-through taxation. This means that earnings of an LLC are taxed only once. The earnings of an LLC are treated like the earnings from partnerships, sole proprietorships, and most S corporations.

- Like general partnerships, LLCs are generally free to establish any organizational structure agreed on by the members. Thus, profit interests may be separated from voting interests.

Disadvantages

- Some states require that a LLC have more than one member

- Legal assistance is required to set up

- More paperwork is necessary than for an ordinary partnership

- Some states require that a dissolution date be listed in the articles of organization. This date may be amended. Further, certain events, such as death of a member, a

122

member leaving, bankruptcy, etc. can be a dissolution event. A corporation has unlimited life, and these events are not dissolution events for a corporation.

- The LLC is a newer entity, and people are not as familiar with the LLC as a corporation.

The Limited Liability Partnership (LLP) is quite similar to a partnership, but allows limited liability for all partners. Appropriate registration and other requirements must be followed.

A Professional Corporation (PC) is much like a corporation or subchapter S Corporation but is regulated as to who can own shares. Usually this form of ownership is limited to licensed professionals in the same profession, such as doctors or lawyers.

A Professional Limited Liability Company (PLLC) is similar to a LLC but is regulated as to who can be members. This form of ownership is usually limited to licensed professionals in the same field, such as doctors, engineers, and lawyers.

In addition to the organization form of ownership, other major legal considerations for a small business are as follows:

- **Issues to address in organizational documents**

  - Procedures for voting
  - Admission of new parties
  - Providing continuity
  - Resolving deadlocks
  - Continuity in the event of death, disability, or bankruptcy of an owner
  - Sources of capital

- **Business issues to consider in structuring a company**

- **Exposure to liability**

  - Product liability
  - Environmental protection

> Errors and omissions
> Fraud allegations
> Worker compensation
> Defamation
> Trademark and copyright infringement

- **Regulatory authorities**

  > Licenses and permits
  > Securities regulation
  > Consumer protection
  > Labor relations
  > Environmental protection

- **Registration with taxing authorities**

  > Federal income taxes
  > Federal employment taxes and withholding
  > State employment taxes
  > Federal excise taxes
  > State sales and use taxes
  > State franchise and excise taxes
  > Miscellaneous state taxes
  > Local general property tax

Franchising has become a popular form of small business ownership. A **franchise** is a licensing agreement between a **franchisor** (the owner of the product or service) and a **franchisee** (the affiliated dealer). When you pay for the right to use an established company's name, product, service, or trade secret, you are buying a franchise. The nature of a franchise relationship can take many forms. In some franchises, the name and product are all you buy. In others, specific regulations are imposed in such areas as building design, price structure, and marketing strategy. Franchising is also a strategy to consider if you are trying to expand to new market areas.

There are many aspects of franchising that make it extremely appealing to prospective business owners. The mere fact that a business is already operating with an established, successful product or service make franchising attractive. Franchise operations generally have a lower risk of failure, as they are offering a consumer-accepted image that sells. Good franchisors offer assistance in all phases of the development of the business, from site location to management and record keeping assistance. This affords the potential franchisee the opportunity to open a business with no previous experience. Although franchise benefits vary from franchise to franchise, many offer national publicity and even financial assistance.

While noting the many advantages of franchising, it is important also to consider its disadvantages. Franchising can be stifling for the true entrepreneur. In many cases, the franchise arrangement forces the franchisee to adhere to specific standards, guidelines, and restrictions imposed by the franchisor. Very often, there is little opportunity for creativity or innovation, as the franchisee is subject to the final say-so of the parent company. This negates the motivation of many true entrepreneurs to be their own boss with the ability to make significant decisions regarding the direction their business should take.

Should you decide franchising is your road to business ownership, it is important that you find a franchise that fits. Franchises are available in almost every form imaginable in almost every industry. Not only should you find a franchise that fits your finances, but also one that fits your personality, lifestyle, and interests. Begin by taking an honest evaluation of yourself. Make sure you are a suitable franchisee, that you understand the nature of the franchise agreement, and can handle the loss of independence. Take a hard look at your qualifications, including your skills, experience, and overall disposition. Although the parent company provides assistance in business development, the success of your franchise will be dependent upon your abilities, energies, and enthusiasm. Building any business is hard work; it requires long hours and dedication.

After you have evaluated your needs and personal resources, make a list of your requirements and investigate available franchise opportunities. Information can be obtained from a number of sources, including libraries, the International Franchise Association, and the U.S. Department of Commerce. When you have found several franchises that fit your requirements, contact the parent company and ask for their "franchise kit." It is important that you do your homework and use good business judgement when choosing a franchise. Read the franchise material carefully and do additional research on the parent company's financial position, reputation, and current franchisees.

In short, a franchised business is much like any other. The success of your individual franchise is, for the most part, totally dependent on your efforts and your determination to succeed. Commonly cited benefits and disadvantages of franchising are highlighted below.

Franchising Benefits

- *Franchising provides a chance to open a business without previous experience.*

- *Franchising often provides a chance to open a business with less capital.*

- *Many franchises provide financial assistance.*

- *Franchises generally have a consumer-accepted image.*

- *Franchises generally offer consistent quality.*

- *Franchising affords combined buying power, allowing for purchasing advantages.*

- *Franchises offer basic training and continued assistance.*

- *Franchises provide location analysis*

- *Franchising provides the financial capability to buy a choice location.*

- *Franchising provides advantageous rental or leasing rates.*

- *Franchisers assist in the development of well-designed facilities, fixtures, and displays, and provide supplies.*

- *Franchisers offer managerial and records assistance.*

- *Franchisers offer sales, advertising, and marketing assistance.*

- *Franchisers generally provide national publicity, promotion, and recognition.*

- *Franchising affords higher income potential.*

- *Franchises have a lower rate of failure.*

- *Franchises provide continual research and development.*

Franchising Disadvantages

Some of the disadvantages of franchising include:

- *The subjugation of personal identity.*

- *The submission to significant standardization and control.*

- *The franchisee does not have the option of selecting the product line.*

Before going into any franchise arrangement, the opportunity needs to be evaluated thoroughly. Checking with an attorney is advisable.

A Franchise Evaluation "How To"

After you have identified several franchise opportunities that fit your personal requirements, it is crucial that you thoroughly evaluate each opportunity before making your final selection. Protection is offered to prospective franchisees through the Federal Trade Commission. The FTC's franchise rule requires every franchisor to provide prospective franchisees with extensive disclosure documents before any contract is signed. These documents should include information on required franchise fees, any bankruptcy or litigation history of the company, a financial statement, earnings claim, and how long the franchise agreement will last. Factors to consider in evaluating a franchise opportunity are highlighted below.

- How long has the firm been in business? What are its reputation and background?

- What is the company's product or service? Is it a staple, a luxury item, or is it seasonal? How long has it been on the market? Is there a market for it in your area? What is the competition? What will demand for the product or service be in the future?

- What is the franchise fee, and what does it cover? What is the total investment required? Are there royalty fees and how much are they?

- Is the firm adequately financed? What kind of financial assistance is offered?

- What training components are offered? Is training ongoing?

- Are franchisees required to buy products or services from the parent company? If so, how are they supplied and priced?

- Does the franchisor assist with site selection? Are there building or space requirements involved?

- Is the franchisee's territory well defined? Does the franchisor offer exclusive rights?

- What advertising, promotion, and marketing assistance does the franchisor provide?

- Does the franchisor offer bookkeeping assistance? Are there accounting or periodic reporting requirements?

- What is the length of the contract? Does the contract include renewal terms or termination clauses?

Go over the company's "franchise kit" carefully and look for answers to the questions previously noted. If you need clarification in any area, contact the company and request further details.

In addition, there are two other crucial details that must be taken care of before a final selection can be made. **First**, be sure to have the franchise agreement examined by an attorney and an accountant. **Second**, make sure you obtain a list of all current franchisees of the company and contact as many as possible. Their experience with the company is invaluable to your evaluation process, as they can offer a clear picture of what to expect from the franchise relationship.

Have you taken the necessary precautions to protect that wonderful name and symbol or logo which perfectly represents the image of your individual business and is seen everywhere your business name appears? What have you done to guard against someone else's having the same logo or even having your business name?

Trademarks are distinctive names or symbols used by a business which distinguish its products from those of another firm. The use and creation of a trademark comprise the first step in making it yours exclusively. The next step is to register your business symbol or trademark with the State Trademark Office, often the Secretary of State. The process of incorporating a business in most states preserves the use of your business name in your industry area. However, if you are not incorporated, you may want to consider registering your name as well as your trademark with The Secretary of State. Obtaining a state trademark is usually painless, very inexpensive, gives you legal rights to the trademark for a designated period of time, and can be renewed.

If your trademark is used in interstate commerce, it can be registered with the U.S. Trademark Office. This registration gives you legal rights for 20 years and can also be renewed. You can handle the registration paperwork yourself, but you may want to have an attorney assist you with this process.

Now, what about your fantastic business plan? Business plans are not patentable, nor are methods of doing business and individual ideas. What is covered under U.S. patent laws are methods of manufacturing, new and useful articles, chemicals, combinations, and improvements thereon.

If you have an invention that is unique and desire a patent, you should contact the U.S. Patent Office for information. General information may be obtained by visiting **www.uspto.gov.**

Legal protection methods include not only patents, trademarks, or service marks, but also copyrights and trade secrets. It is best to consult an attorney if you have intellectual property concerns. Additional information about copyrights may be obtained by visiting the government's copyright Web site, **www.copyright.gov**. Trademark information is available at **www.uspto.gov**.

All businesses need to consider intellectual property issues and address legal methods of protection. This is an area that all too often goes overlooked by entrepreneurial leaders.

Details, Details, Details.

"Pay attention to the details even though it may seem

that you are spending too much time on them.

Excellence is in the details."

M.G.L.J.

Section VII

Go, Team, Go !!

The Human Side of the Enterprise

"It's very difficult to find good, capable, dependable,

honest employees. It's even harder to keep them.

Take time to praise and cherish your

most valuable resources."

M.G.L.J.

The successful, globally minded entrepreneurial leader has learned the art of developing a skilled team. The competitive 21st Century leader cannot afford to continually drain all of her or his energy trying to wear all of the company hats, but must focus on recruiting the best people with specific skills and expertise to propel the firm into the new era. Historically, small businesses had difficulty in finding and luring top people away from big companies. Now as big corporations are re-engineering, small businesses have a broader personnel pool of displaced, skilled corporate personnel. Additionally, thanks to modern technology, new recruitment venues are available.

Now, where do we find these talented individuals? The Internet has tremendously expanded the entrepreneur's employee candidate base from their immediate locality to the world. Using the World Wide Web network bulletin boards, the entrepreneur can advertise a position to a wide range of individuals who are already progressive enough to be job hunting on the Web. Also, state employment offices are now posting positions on the American Job Bank on the Internet. And, of course, small businesses can post position openings on their own Web site. Corporate outplacement services, along with search firms, private personnel agencies, or corporate headhunters in a specific industry, are also effective recruitment venues. These firms can help the entrepreneur locate the best candidates in a particular field. Leading institutions of higher education offering business, entrepreneurial education and training in specific industry areas are sources of a broad range of potential employees. Such institutions have young, talented people eager to learn and gain a variety of experiences which are often uniquely offered by the small business arena. Institutions of higher education are also a haven for older experienced adults who are re-equipping themselves with skills for a new age and are willing and able to take on new challenges. Advertising through industry trade journals will also help the entrepreneur find individuals in tune with a specific industry and with industry-specific skills. And yes, let us not forget the value of "word of mouth" recruitment and newspaper ads. If you're in the right circles, this can prove to be valuable in locating individuals who already come with a recommendation in hand.

Choosing and affording the right team for a small business is not an easy task. In fact, it may mean that the entrepreneur has to make hard and fast compromises, often diverting money from other aspects of the firm to salaries and benefits. Recent studies have found that compensation is one of the main reasons individuals turn down positions and that many potential recruits turn jobs down if retirement benefits are not offered.

Yes, all of the ultimate challenges and responsibilities rest on the head of the entrepreneur; but in order to grow, the globally competitive entrepreneur must share the hats and recruit and develop a skilled winning team.

People are a business's most important asset. Recruit good people, manage their talents with management savvy and sensitivity, and your business assets will multiply; but do your employees really know what you expect of them?

Before you can think about hiring an additional vital asset, it is important to first determine the functions and reporting responsibilities of each person holding a position in your firm. It's up to you to decide how you want your business structured and who will make the best employee for each job. Hire only those persons who can lend strength to your organization and write formal job descriptions for all of your personnel. In addition to helping you focus your ideas, the description will provide employees with objectives to be achieved as well as a clear understanding of your expectations of them.

A typical job description should include the following parts:

- ***HEADER:*** *Identifies the job title, title of the immediate supervisor, and location within the organization.*

- ***PRINCIPAL PURPOSE:*** *Presents a summary of the job description, placing it in context with the rest of the organization.*

- ***PRINCIPAL RESPONSIBILITIES:*** *Lists responsibilities in priority sequence, showing the percentage of time to be spent on each responsibility area.*

- ***JOB SKILLS:*** *Lists specific prerequisite knowledge, skills, education, or training necessary for fulfilling the responsibilities of the position.*

- ***SCOPE:*** *Quantifies areas of authority, such as the number of people supervised.*

The development and availability of affordable technology, including computers, interactive distance technology, fax machines, and modems, afford the 21st Century entrepreneur the opportunity to create satellite work stations for home-based contract employees. Thus, employees don't have to commute; they telecommute.

Home-based contract employees, or home-based business owners, offer services needed by many small and large businesses alike. They represent a growing trend and tremendous savings for the entrepreneur without sacrificing quality. Services can include mail order processing, mass mailings, marketing assistance, customer service, making sales calls, bill collection, secretarial support, general business support, and technology support. Professionals in their own right, the home-based contract employees need no job training except familiarization with your business. They usually have their own equipment and require no benefit package, thus waiving costs of unemployment insurance, disability, social security, paid sick leave, paid vacations, and health care. The entrepreneur also saves by only paying for work performed, be it work on a one-time project or routine work.

Finding an independent contractor shouldn't be difficult. Check phone books, local chambers, professional, home-based contract associations, friends, and other organizations.

This new frontier, representing workers linked to your business by modern technology, eliminates many overhead expenses for the progressive entrepreneur, not to mention assisting in strengthening the small business sector of our economy. As we proceed in the 21st Century, "don't commute, telecommute" may quite possibly become the buzz slogan.

"I can't find good employees" is a common cry of many entrepreneurs. It is up to the progressive entrepreneur to address creatively this dilemma. One way to circumvent this problem may be right at your back door.

Consider looking at neighboring colleges and universities for a young and vibrant personnel pool which is able and willing to work at minimal to no cost. Many college disciplines require or encourage students to get practical experience as interns in their field. What better way to get experience than to work in a small business where the student is called upon to learn so much in varied aspects of the business? On the entrepreneurial side, what better way to encourage college graduates to consider entrepreneurship as a career option than to take young talent under your wings and at the same time expand your personnel resource base?

Interns come to the world of work with a fresh and eager viewpoint. They want and need practical experience and a chance to test their knowledge. Most are not expecting money, just a chance to test the waters and make contacts in their selected field. The entrepreneur gets a chance to groom a young, willing mind and to watch the intern blossom into a professional, not to mention the possibility of grooming a future full-time employee.

Internship programs of course vary widely from campus to campus and from discipline to discipline, but the basic goals are the same: To provide practical, hands-on training for which the student often receives college credit. Some internship programs require the business to pay a nominal wage, some schools pay the intern a salary, while other schools expect students to receive no compensation.

139

Interns should not be viewed as a cheap source of labor to perform menial tasks, nor should they be led to believe that the internship will result in full-time employment upon graduation. Employers of course need to screen interns thoroughly and find a good match, just as you would with any potential employee; and agreements should be understood by both parties on the front end as to what is and isn't expected. Entrepreneurs also have to understand that an intern has a class schedule that must be taken into consideration in terms of work hours and schedule.

When you elect to groom young college, or even high school talent, both parties win. The entrepreneur ends up with a trained potential employee already in tune with the company's philosophies and methods of operating, and the intern gets practical experience and a basis to make appropriate career choices.

If you are interested in investigating internship possibilities, contact the career placement center at local colleges and universities or the university discipline most closely related to your type of business.

All too often, business leaders assume that all adults know how to behave in the business arena so that a topic as elementary as conduct is never discussed when hiring new employees. Certainly, discussing behavior perhaps sounds very condescending; but if you have ever visited a small business where employees did not look or act professional or one where employees seemed to have never heard about customer service, you know that behavior is a topic that requires management attention.

The entrepreneurial leader must set the tone of the business, including acceptable and unacceptable behavior for each employee. Every organization has its own unique climate. The climate includes the emotional overtones, attitudes, and behaviors of the people in the organization along with the overall ethical posturing of the firm. New employees should not only feel that climate but also must know what is expected of them when operating in the unique environment you have created.

A Code of Conduct should be designed to let employees know your expectations of them, along with appropriate behaviors in the work environment and acceptable behavior when certain types of situations arise. Be it keeping lunch to an hour, being honest, being a team player, not playing music in the office, or guidelines for dealing with irate clients, your professional and work standards of behavior should be in writing and also communicated orally. The Code of Conduct should be work-focused but can also include outside activities that may impact the business, such as not using the company name in conjunction with political activities.

Remember that employees actually desire to know what is expected of them. At the same time, realize that employees mirror the attitudes and integrity of their leader. So, in order to lead and guide behavior, the entrepreneurial leader cannot afford to operate outside of the rules established for others.

If you define motivation as energy or drive that mobilizes people toward achieving goals, then true motivation comes from within. If, however, you define a motivator as a person who influences other people, helps them reach a goal, provides incentives for success, and creates an environment in which goals are achieved, then yes, you can be a motivator.

Yes, you can motivate if you understand what "floats your employees' boats." You need to learn what people want for themselves and what they're willing to give in order to get what they want or need. In this way, you'll know which rewards will work to motivate employees.

Some basic "givens" also need to be linked to motivation on the part of employees. Employees have to want to do their jobs and do them well; they have to be capable of doing their jobs or learning how to do them, and they have to understand what they have to do and the standards by which their work will be judged.

The entrepreneurial leader also needs a basic understanding of the common payoffs people actually want from work. Research shows that what really motivates employees, listed in descending order, are: job security, high wages, full appreciation for work performed, a feeling of being in on things, interesting work, good working conditions, promotion opportunities, tactful discipline, sympathetic help on personal problems, and the personal loyalty of their supervisor.

Yes, you can develop a motivated work force. You first need to know your behavior deficits. Then, you need employees who are ready and willing to accept stimuli. If you figure out what "floats their boats" and create a productive and encouraging work environment void of obstacles and barriers to their performance, your employees can help make you a leadership success story. Remember, each employee is an individual with unique and distinctive personal goals, values, and needs. Review the following lists and use them as a guide as you evaluate each of your employees to determine what will float their boats.

WHAT FLOATS YOUR TEAM MEMBERS' BOATS?

Why Are They Members of the Team?

- **Believe in the Organization's Mission**

- **Prestige**

- **Want To Belong**

- **Need A Salary**

- **Need Something To Do**

- _____

- _____

What Rewards Are Valued?

- **Praise**

- **Public Recognition**

- **Challenging Work**

- **A Title**

- **A Raise**

- _____

- _____

- _____

144

A common complaint among entrepreneurial leaders is the difficulty in finding, keeping, and motivating good employees. This is a very valid complaint. The ability to retain good employees and keep them motivated, however, may in fact relate to the personality of the entrepreneur.

It is often believed that leaders are either **aggressive** or **assertive** in terms of behavior by the mere fact that they have taken the initiative to lead and/or start a business. Working under the belief that there is a lot of merit in this assessment, it becomes important to note the impact of aggressive and assertive behavior on employee performance.

Aggressive leaders, while they feel powerful, energetic, and in charge, also eventually find that they lose good employees. Very aggressive individuals tend to show little respect for the needs of others; they focus on satisfying their own needs and taking advantage of others. This makes employees feel angry, threatened, frustrated, anxious, defensive, tired, and resentful, and they will eventually leave the company.

On the other hand, **assertive** leaders are those who have a realistic concern for themselves but also a concern for the needs and feelings of those around them. They are positive, calm, in control, energetic, honest, direct, and confident. Assertive entrepreneurs tend to make employees feel secure, positive, respected, and energetic, leading to a more motivated and dedicated employee base.

To Thine Own Self Be True. You need to step back and assess your behavior. The ability to motivate effectively and lead employees is based largely on the entrepreneurial leader's behavior and the behavioral patterns of his or her employees. The following chart provides valuable insight in assessing how your behavior impacts others and how they interact with you.

STYLES OF BEHAVIOR
AND
THEIR EFFECTS

BEHAVIOR	PASSIVE AND SOCIALLY COMPLIANT	AGGRESSIVE	*ASSERTIVE*
DESCRIPTION OF BEHAVIOR	SACRIFICE YOUR OWN NEEDS FOR THE NEEDS OF OTHERS	SHOW LITTLE RESPECT FOR THE NEEDS OF OTHERS; SATISFY YOUR OWN NEEDS AND HURT OTHERS; TAKE ADVANTAGE OF OTHERS	HAVE A REALISTIC CONCERN FOR YOURSELF BUT ALSO CONCERN FOR THE NEEDS AND FEELINGS OF THOSE AROUND YOU
HOW PEOPLE WITH THE BEHAVIOR OFTEN FEEL ABOUT THEMSELVES	ANGRY, FRUSTRATED, WITHDRAWN, INSECURE, INFERIOR, ANXIOUS, DEFEATED, UNABLE TO ACKNOWLEDGE FEELINGS	POWERFUL, GUILTY, THREATENED, ALWAYS RIGHT, CRITICAL, LONELY, EXCESSIVELY ENERGETIC	POSITIVE, CALM, ENTHUSIASTIC, PROUD, HONEST, DIRECT, CONFIDENT, SATISFIED, IN CONTROL, ABLE TO ACKNOWLEDGE FEELINGS, RESPECT FOR OTHERS, ENERGETIC
HOW PEOPLE WITH THE BEHAVIOR MAKE OTHER PEOPLE FEEL	IRRITATED, WITHDRAWN, SUPERIOR, TIRED	ANGRY, THREATENED, FRUSTRATED, WITHDRAWN, ANXIOUS, DEFENSIVE, RESENTFUL, HURT, HUMILIATED, TIRED	POSITIVE, SECURE, COOPERATIVE, RESPECTFUL, ENERGETIC

146

Anatagonology is the art and skill of dealing with difficult people and those difficult, stressful, gut-wrenching situations that leaders face.

DIFFICULT PEOPLE ARE THE . . . .

⇒ hostile/angry/belligerent

⇒ pushy/presumptuous/arrogant

⇒ underhanded/deceptive

⇒ shrewd/manipulative/exploitative

⇒ discourteous

⇒ egotistical/self-centered/self-seeking

⇒ procrastinating/vacillating/delaying

people of the world.

DIFFICULT PEOPLE . . . .

⇒ make you look bad because of their poor performance

⇒ make you lose your control

⇒ force you to do things you don't want to do

⇒ use coercion, manipulation

DIFFICULT PEOPLE . . . .

⇒ arouse your guilt complex when you don't go along with their program

⇒ make you feel anxious, upset, frustrated, angry, depressed, envious, etc.

⇒ make you do their share of the work

Difficult people can cause conflict. An effective way to look at coping with conflict is to assess the importance of the relationship involved in the conflict situation. The strategy an effective leader uses to resolve conflict is based on the importance of the relationship and the priority of the goal. The following chart provides a guide for selecting the appropriate strategy to bring about effective conflict resolution.

	Importance of the Relationship	Importance of the Goal	Strategies
1	Low	High	Confront, Dominate, Persist, Control
2	Low	Low	Ignore, Concede, Deny, Withdraw
3	Medium	Medium	Compromise, Negotiate
4	High	Low	Supress, Accommodate, Avoid
5	High	High	Integrate, Collaborate

Employee theft, one of the silent killers of small business, is a persistent problem for small firms. The problem is perhaps magnified by the fact that many small firms do not choose or are not able to pay top wages. Thus, some employees think their stealing is justified to compensate for their low salaries. Even employees stealing paper, pens, staplers, and software for home use impact the bottom line.

Internal crime can take on many forms. It could be the disappearance of merchandise; the selling of merchandise to friends at astronomically low prices; the stealing of money, supplies, or business secrets; or the capture of clients and customers to start a new employee-related venture. The signs of employee theft are as varied as the forms of crime. Some common signs of employee theft include bounced company checks, missing records and merchandise, large miscellaneous payments, managers performing clerical duties, employee drug abuse, and business records reflecting a profit figure that just doesn't seem right. And yes, that gut vibe that an employee is not honest is another indicator.

In order for entrepreneurial leaders to protect themselves from employee theft, certain measures should be taken to decrease risk. The first step is to hire right. Employers should check out new hires through stringent reference contacts. Many firms also utilize integrity or honesty tests. Honesty tests can be administered to potential employees as a gauge for their propensity to steal, but of course, a thief is also likely to lie on such a test. Financial controls are a must and should be enforced through tight organizational policies. One person being in charge of all financial duties will create a higher risk for the business, as there is just too much room for playing with numbers. All financial duties should be performed by one person and double-checked by another. Using an outside professional auditor might also be advisable.

Additionally, employers need to create a climate of honesty which first must be set by example, not only in the business but also in dealing with customers. Simultaneously, employers should keep a watchful eye on the business, establish and maintain stringent policies, and learn to evaluate financial records. Employers also need to realize that when extreme internal theft situations arise, the services of an outside investigator may be warranted.

Employee theft is not just limited to tangible items. Trade secrets and sensitive business information are also candidates for the take. Recognizing that unique processes, strategies, and creative strategic plans may be the small business owner's competitive edge in the market, securing this information is vital.

Shoplifting is another common problem that poses a threat to profitability in retailing, but such a serious security issue is beyond the scope of this publication. Consultation with a security specialist is recommended for devising an adequate protection plan and providing appropriate employee training.

Even though *ethics* is a popular buzzword in business circles, internal crime is still alive and well, casting a negative veil on the profit line for many small and struggling firms. It is difficult enough for small businesses to compete with larger firms or stores, but overlooking the significance of employee theft on the bottom line can eventually lead to the silent death of a potentially successful business.

Employees, one of every organization's most valuable resources, can make your organization go and grow. One good way to stifle a firm's growth is to become consumed in human relations problems and internal disgruntlement. Discontent is often the fault of the entrepreneur who lacks basic positive communication and human relations skills. The following suggestions are provided to help you get the most from your employees and enhance your firm's growth potential.

TEN COMMANDMENTS FOR GETTING THE MOST FROM EMPLOYEES

1. *Think through the ramifications and repercussions of what you are getting ready to say before you say it.*

2. *Pay attention not only to what you say but also to how you say it. Tactfully select your words and tone.*

3. *Make promises sparingly and keep them faithfully.*

4. *Don't overlook opportunities to say kind and encouraging words.*

5. *Show a sincere interest in employees: their pursuits, their homes and families.*

6. *Be cheerful.*

7. *Keep an open mind and consider the opinions of employees.*

8. *Never respond or react to comments made by an employee about other employees.*

9. *Learn to listen carefully and pay full attention to other's thoughts and words.*

10. *Respond to the requests of employees in a timely and considerate manner. What you view as an insignificant request may relate to the most important aspect of an employee's life.*

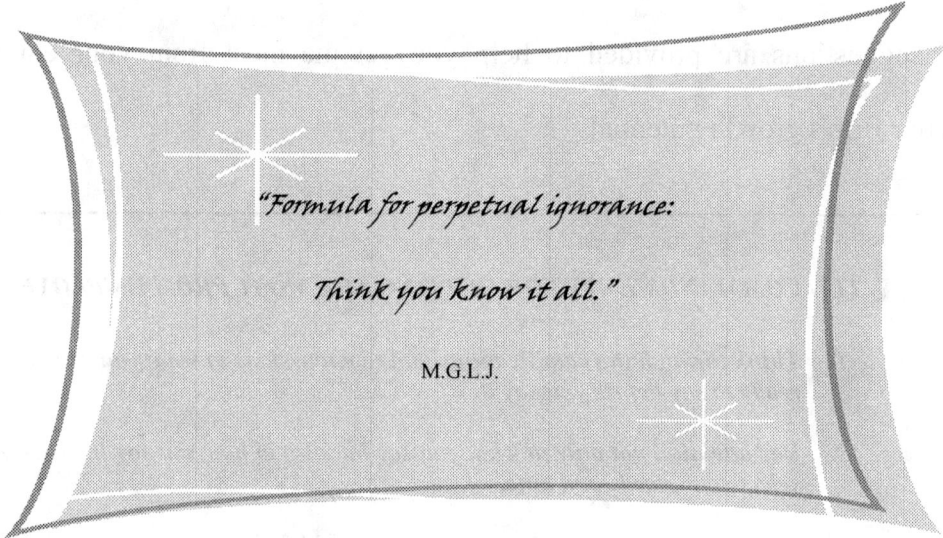

"Formula for perpetual ignorance:

Think you know it all."

M.G.L.J.

Section VIII

Success Soup for the Savvy Soul

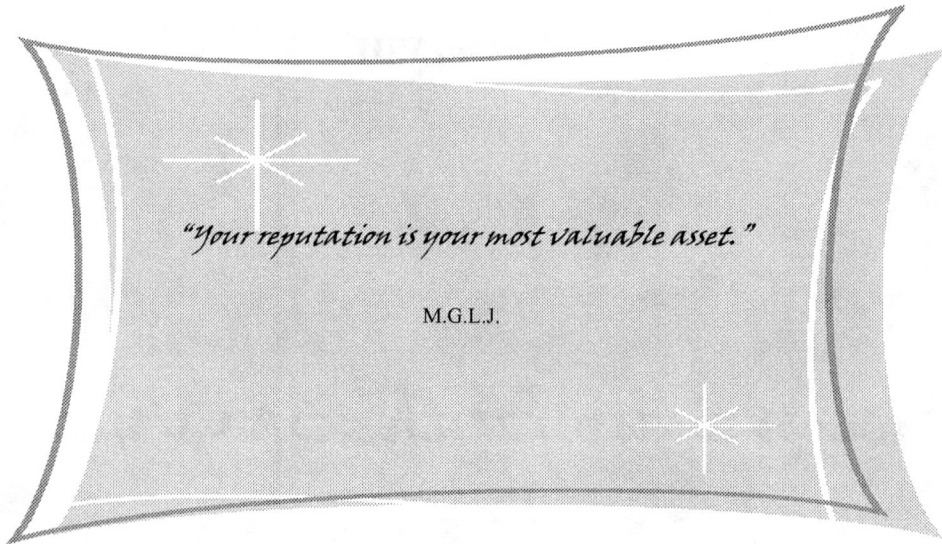

"Your reputation is your most valuable asset."

M.G.L.J.

So you have risen to a position of leadership--a position of authority, status, power, and unbelievable responsibility. You have risen to a position encompassing unwavering challenges.

Leaders are a special breed that thrive on stress. They live dangerously and expect to be judged by their results; taking daily calculated risks is a way of life. This "good" stress (eustress) keeps us leader types moving and achieving. But too much of a good thing can kill you. Stress, the inner time bomb in leaders that keeps us going, could easily be ignited and could explode.

You cannot avoid stress. In fact, you would be pretty bored without a certain amount of it. Stress gives us motivation and enables us to perform at our peak. The key is to increase your ability to identify stressors that bring on too much "bad" stress (distress) and take control of your life by responding appropriately. Without taking control, you may find yourself victimized by many illnesses including **headaches, ulcers, strokes, high blood pressure, heart attacks, or even death.**

Each of us experiences stress differently. Stress may be seen and felt in many different ways. It has even been found that Type A personalities--the time–pressured, aggressive, often angry people – put themselves under constant stress.

But what are the signs that indicate the potential detonation of your inner time bomb signaling impending health problems brought on by the mere responsibilities of being a leader? These signals are highlighted on the next page for your careful reflection.

STRESS WARNING SIGNALS

Emotional signals: apathy, anxiety, irritability, mental fatigue, lack of concentration

Behavioral signals: avoidance, the urge to cry, run, or hide, extreme responses

Physical signals: inability to sleep, indigestion, increased smoking, increased alcohol, lower back pain, neck pain, headaches, physical exhaustion, weight loss or gain, loss of sex drive, pounding of heart, increased use of drugs or medicine.

If you recognize that you are experiencing a significant number of potential detonation signals, you need to start taking action immediately to alleviate some of your stressors. Take time to relax, practice stress alleviation techniques, and make sure you get a yearly physical. In other words, take some time out for you or you may never see your leadership vision become a reality.

The following listings provide useful stress-management techniques. First, several coping strategies are identified, followed by "rules" for achieving happiness.

Strategies for Coping with Stress

✓ Identify stressors and anticipate their occurrence.

✓ Set realistic goals for yourself.

✓ Look at stressful situations realistically.

✓ Acknowledge that some stress can't be helped.

✓ Learn to say NO without feeling guilty.

✓ Give in occasionally.

✓ Learn to accept what you cannot change.

✓ Learn to communicate effectively.

✓ Exercise regularly.

✓ Pay attention to good nutrition.

✓ Practice relaxation.

✓ Talk about your concerns with someone you trust.

✓ Practice positive self-talks.

✓ Organize your time, make lists, and set priorities.

✓ Keep your humor. Humor is a great stress reliever.

TEN RULES FOR HAPPIER LIVING

1. Pray (or you will lose your way).

2. Do a kindness (and forget it).

3. Give something away (no strings attached).

4. Look intently into the face of a baby (and marvel).

5. Laugh often (it's life's lubricant).

6. Work (with vim and vigor).

7. Plan as though you'll live forever.

8. Live as though you'll die tomorrow (because you will die on some tomorrow).

9. Spend a few minutes with the aged (their experience is a priceless guidance).

10. Give thanks (a thousand times a day is not enough).

Author Unknown

Are you "time locked?" You're stressed and frustrated because you can't possibly squeeze another second out of your schedule. Your responsibilities and commitments are overwhelming, and you don't even know what fun and relaxation are anymore. Just as gridlock stops traffic, "timelock" stops productivity and stifles creativity. Here are some pointers to unlock your life and your time.

- *Assess you calendar and all of your activities. If they add to your life or your business plan, keep them; if not, eliminate them.*

- *Learn to understand your body clock. Schedule important tasks and meetings at your peak time of the day.*

- *Don't crowd every minute of the day with some task; your stress and tension will rise and your effectiveness will decline.*

- *Slow down; avoid the entrepreneurial tendency to be hurried; don't be addicted to rushing; subtract an old activity when you add a new one.*

If you're really ready to commit to making the most of your time and life, you will need to take decisive action to unlock your time. De-locking your time will increase your effectiveness and decrease your stress while simultaneously allowing you to begin attaining some level of inner peace.

The savvy entrepreneurial leader--the leader with vision, goals, determination, creative ideas, and the guts to make things happen--must know appropriate business etiquette in order to be taken seriously as a professional. The following tips and guidelines are provided to position you above the pack and propel you to higher levels.

Business Dining

At the dining table, remember these basic guidelines.

- Your solid items, such as your salad and bread plate, will be found to the left of your dinner setting.
- Your water and beverages will be found to the right of your dinner setting
- Place the napkin in your lap as soon as you are seated. When you have completed your meal, place the napkin, neatly folded, on the table to the left of your plate. If you must leave the table momentarily while dining, place your napkin on the chair.
- When you have several utensils, the utensil farthest from your plate will be the utensil you use for the first course; and you continue using utensils for different courses moving from the outside inward.
- Don't eat until everyone at the table is served. In a banquet or any dining situation, always wait until everyone at the table has been served before you begin your meal. When they see that their not being served is holding up everyone from getting started with their meal, those who have savvy etiquette will tell other diners at the table to feel free to get started. To keep someone who starts eating before you are served from embarrassing themselves, tell everyone at the table to go ahead and begin their meal without you.
- When eating meat, always cut and eat one small piece at a time.
- When served bread, break the bread with your fingers into pieces small enough for one or two bites. Butter one small piece at a time. Never butter an entire piece of bread or a roll at one time, and remember to leave your bread on your bread plate if one is provided.
- Never talk with your mouth full
- Food should be passed to the right.

> **Dining Basics**
>
> ◆
>
> **Left--solids**
>
> **Right--liquids**
>
> **Use utensils from the outside in.**
>
> **Don't eat until everyone at the table is served.**

160

- When you complete a meal, place the knife and fork parallel to one another across the plate with the knife blade facing inward toward the plate. Place the knife and fork in the position of ten to four o'clock or straight across at the top of the plate.

- If you are at a banquet and the place setting has a coffee cup, simply turn your cup upside down if you don't care to be served coffee. This tells the waiter that you don't desire coffee.

- When ordering wine at an exclusive restaurant where there is a wine steward, the wine steward will show you the wine bottle. You should read the label and note if the label is correct for the wine you have ordered. You may also be given the cork to check for moisture; if so, pinch it. The steward will pour a small amount of wine in a glass. If it is red wine, you sniff the wine for the bouquet. (White wine is not sniffed for bouquet.) Sip the wine; let it roll slowly over your tongue and nod approval if all is well.

Dining at a Private Home

- It is appropriate to take a small host or hostess gift
- Arrive no less than 10 to 15 minutes after the appointed time
- Drink moderately
- Praise the host or hostess
- Send a thank you note to your host or hostess

On The Personal Side

- Choose friends wisely and keep your friends and your network to yourself
- Start investing as soon as possible
- Tip appropriately
- Don't over indulge (food or drink)
- Be involved in community, civic, and social organizations
- Learn to golf or learn the sport the powerful people play in your environment
- Learn stress alleviation techniques

Tips on Tipping
◆

Tip servers 15- 20% of the bill

Tip the wine steward $3.00 to $5.00 per bottle

Tip a restroom attendant $1.00

When traveling, tip the hotel/motel attendants, taxi driver, and tour guide.

161

- Never let insurance lapse (car, property, health, disability, and life)
- Avoid the debt trap and keep a good credit rating
- Keep your spirituality in order

Effective Business Communication

Techno-Etiquette:

- Answering the Phone
  Your answering technique conveys an image of both you and your company; make sure that you reflect a good image. This is a caller's first, and often lasting, impression.

  When you answer the phone and the caller asks for you by name, you should respond, "**this is she" or "this is he**," not "this is her" or "this is him."

- Voice Mail
  Voice mail messages make first and lasting impressions. Take time to strategically develop voice mail messages

- Cell Phones and Pagers
  Use courtesy and discretion

- Speaker Phone
  Many are offended by being placed on a speaker phone conversation

The Power of the Word:

- Correspondence
  Use appropriate grammar in all correspondence. If necessary, have a close friend proof your writing. Don't be too proud to take a refresher course in grammar or buy a grammar book and study. Poor grammar implies limited education and knowledge. Poor grammar can quickly negate all of your other savvy skills and qualities.

  When writing letters or reports, refer to a standard writing style manual for appropriate format.

Take time to word correspondence carefully for the desired intent and response. Don't become frustrated because it is taking too much time to get the wording correct in a letter. An important letter may take quite a bit of time to formulate effectively.

- E-Mail

    Take time to proof all e-mails you transmit. Hurriedly produced e-mails often contain simplistic grammar and typing errors which subtly send a message of carelessness or even ignorance to the receiver. Also be conscious of your e-mail address. Don't use an address such as hotlips@hotmail.com.

- The Spoken Word

    The importance of appropriate grammar cannot be stated enough. Take time to formulate what you say before you speak and think about the ramifications and repercussions of your statements. Also, please, please, please, remember that generally the word at should not end a question. (e.g., It is incorrect grammar to ask, Where are my keys at?)

General Protocol Thoughts for Business Settings

- If you are on time, you are late. Always arrive to meetings and appointments early
- Don't discuss religion, politics, sexual, societal/cultural issues
- Don't assume you should call business associates by their first name. Permission should be given by the person. Also, don't decide to give someone a nickname, such as calling Robert by Bob or Millicent by Millie. Always use professional titles, such as Dr., as appropriate. Individuals who have worked hard to obtain their titles are often offended when they are not addressed or referred to properly.
- Dress and act like you are in charge
- Control your consumption of alcoholic beverages
- Don't hover over a buffet table, and don't eat like it is your last meal
- Don't get too personal in conversations
- Perfume, cologne, and aftershave should be used sparingly.
- Don't interrupt someone on the phone or stand near their office when they are on the phone
- Don't bring a casual date to the office party or bring someone to a party or activity uninvited
- Learn to listen and not talk too much

- Keep personal business to yourself
- Respect personal space
- When making introductions, mention the name of the person of authority or importance first. {e.g., "Ms. Martin (the president or vice president), may I present Mr. Jones (division head)."}

Looking the Part

- Dress professionally for the situation. Don't wear suggestive clothing (too much skin exposed, too much cleavage showing, tight clothing, or short skirts). You represent your business and yourself at all times. Never let your guard down.
- Professionals don't chew gum

✓ Develop a "total product" desired by the appropriate target market.

✓ Please your customers.

- Learn their likes and dislikes and make them feel that you are interested.

- Given an extra bit of service, people will tell others.

- It is the little things that count and that give your clients or customers that "warm and fuzzy" feeling, and keeps them coming back.

- Tell the truth about your service even if it means losing a sale. Telling the truth will make that "would be" customer feel that you are an honest businessperson, and they will perhaps patronize you later or tell others.

- Build a positive image. Use a steady promotion plan and be consistent in everything you do.

✓ Encourage teamwork.

- Make employees feel that they are important to your business.

- Praise employees in public; correct them in private.

- Send your staff to workshops and seminars periodically. The knowledge obtained will allow them to benefit your organization more; and at the same time, it will elevate their feeling of worth to you and your organization.

✓ Plan ahead.

✓ Keep expenses in line and make a profit. Determine your break-even point.

✓ Be involved in civic and community affairs. This is free advertising. Do benevolent community deeds which will bring a positive valence to your firm.

✓ Keep your firm's name in the public's eye.

- Always carry your business cards and brochures.

- Have your business checks imprinted with your logo and a descriptive statement about your business. Checks pass through the hands of many individuals who may be in your target market.

✓ Interact and socialize with people who can help you with your business concerns. "It's not what you know; it's who you know." This is an old cliche, but it is quite true in the world of small business. Particularly get to know a banker, lawyer, accountant, marketing/promotion specialist, local politicians, news media representatives, leaders of business, civic, service, political, educational, religious, and professional organizations, and the decision makers of the companies with whom you do business. You may also want to consider joining your local Chamber of Commerce. Remember, when greeting people, always use a firm, confident handshake with direct eye contact and a friendly smile.

✓ Establish yourself as an authority in your field or industry. Use your contacts and get on the guest lecture circuit, talk shows, and community programs. You may even want to teach a class in your field as a part of the continuing education program of a local college. You may have to offer your teaching free initially, but the benefits derived will be great.

✓ Establish credibility for yourself and your business. Provide a good service at an acceptable price and back up your product with guarantees and warranties. Live up to the commitments you make.

✓ Surround yourself with people who know more than you do. Hire staff personnel whose areas of expertise will enable you to expand your knowledge as well as expand your business.

✓ Establish and maintain good credit. Pay your bills on time. If you can't pay on time, call your creditor and see what other arrangements can be made. Keeping cash flow concerns in mind, establish a feasible credit policy for customers and clients.

✓ Take advantage of early payment discounts and quantity discounts whenever possible.

✓ Always represent your business in a very professional manner.

- You are your business, and people will evaluate your business based on you. Your personal appearance is very important at all times, even on Saturday morning in the grocery store. Always wear clothes that are appropriate for your business field and that make you feel that you look good. You feel and act like you look.

So, you have decided that you really want to be an effective and successful entrepreneurial leader. Well, if you are really serious about entrepreneurial leadership, you need a plan. Not just a business plan, but also a well-thought-out strategy that will map out your personal course for leadership success. The format for a leadership action plan which follows will assist you in developing your personal leadership plan for fulfilling your dreams and aspirations of being a successful millentrepreneurial leader.

In developing your leadership plan for action, you must first begin with vision. Think about it. Do you see you and your business featured on the front cover of Business Week, and/or do you see yourself being interviewed on Oprah for the phenomenal success of your business or for the wonderful work of the social entrepreneurial venture you started? Or, do you see yourself simply being honored by your employees for your extraordinary leadership abilities? At the end of this earthly journey, what successes do you want to have achieved? What do you want to be known for as your contribution to society? Write down your leadership vision and claim it. Your leadership vision does not have to be limited to the business or entrepreneurial environment. Also think about leadership roles you may want to assume in community and civic organizations to make a difference.

Next, take time to assess what you bring to the entrepreneurial leadership table. What are your skill sets? What assets and knowledge do you have? What are your contacts and resources? Then think about what knowledge, skills, assets, and resources are needed to accomplish your vision. In comparing what you bring to the table with what is needed to accomplish your goal, answer the following questions. Do I have what it takes to fulfill my vision? Do I have leadership-skill shortcomings or behavior shortcomings that I need to overcome?

After you engage in a thorough assessment of your leadership style and behavior and address personal behavioral patterns that may need to be refined for entrepreneurial leadership success, then it's time to delineate your action steps to fulfill your vision. Identifying action steps without a timeline for completion is merely an academic endeavor, so make sure you develop a timeframe for accomplishing your action steps and also identify factors that could curtail your success as well as ensure your success.

Finally, make an unwavering, serious commitment to stay on track, to fulfill your entrepreneurial leadership vision, and to be a savvy leader.

A guide to assist you in developing your personal leadership plan for action is included on the next page. The leadership plan for action is followed by guideposts for being a successful savvy leader.

*Leadership Plan
for Action*

Date:_____

What Is Your Leadership Vision?
Write it! Critique it! Claim It!

What knowledge, skills, tools, resources, and assets do you need to achieve this goal?

Knowledge:

Skills:

Tools:

Resources:

Assets:

Self-critique your leadership style and behavior.

What do you need to start doing?

What do you need to stop doing?

What do you need to continue doing?

Indicate your action steps and timeline to fulfill your vision.

Action Steps: **Timeline:**

What factors (external and internal) could…

curtail your success?

ensure your success?

To Be A Savvy Leader...

S	Begin with the **SPIRIT**
A	Be **ASTUTE** with business knowledge, organization skills, and management **ACUMEN**
V	Look into the future with **VISION**
V	**VIVACIOUSLY** create a climate based on **VALUES** and think **VICTORIOUSLY**
Y	**YEARN** for excellence and success with unwavering commitment
L	**LEVERAGE** your **LEADERSHIP** skills in producing more leaders, not more followers
E	Be **ENTERPRISING** and **ENTREPRENEURIAL** with a desire to **EMPOWER** others to assist in accomplishing the vision
A	Be **ACTION-ORIENTED, ACCOUNTABLE,** and engage in a process of incessant **ASSESSMENT** for continuous improvement
D	Be **DELIBERATE** in your actions and move with **DETERMINATION** and **DIGNITY**
E	Be **ENTHUSIASTIC** and **ENCOURAGE** others to lead
R	Be **RESULTS-ORIENTED** and **RESILIENT,** with a keen understanding of the importance of **RELATIONSHIPS** and **RESPECT**
S	**STRATEGICALLY** plan with **SOPHISTICATION** and **STYLE**
H	Be **HONEST** and **HONORABLE**
I	Be **INSPIRATIONAL, INTUITIVE,** display **INTEGRITY** in all of your actions, and approach situations with **INGENUITY**
P	Be **PREPARED** for the unexpected

LEADERSHIP IS... THE UNIQUE ABILITY TO GIVE PEOPLE THE DESIRE TO FOLLOW

Are your attitude and mind-set in order to beat out the competition and win in the race for entrepreneurial leadership success? In other words: Are you a Winner or a Loser?

The Winner vs. The Loser

The Winner approaches business with a passion;

The Loser limits passion to the bedroom;

The Winner always has a plan of action along with a back-up plan;

The Loser has no plan;

The Winner knows success only precedes work in the dictionary;

The Loser believes success should come overnight;

The Winner sees an obstacle as a challenge to try new strategies;

The Loser sees an obstacle or pitfall as a hurdle too high to jump;

The Winner dares to dream;

The loser dares only to provide excuses;

The Winner believes that if it's conceivable, it's achievable;

The Loser doesn't even know how to conceive;

The Winner knows when to ask the right questions;

The Loser knows all of the answers.

Dr. Millicent Gray Lownes-Jackson

"Tough times don't last, but tough women do."

M.G.L.J.

LEADERSHIP RESOURCES

BOOKS

Bennis, Warren. (1998). <u>Organizing Genius</u>. Cambridge, MA: Perseus Publishing

Bennis, Warren. (1994). <u>On Becoming a Leader</u>. Cambridge, MA: Perseus Publishing.

Bennis, Warren. (1977). <u>Leaders</u>. New York: Harper Business

Blanchard, Hodges. (2003). <u>The Servant Leader</u>. Nashville: Thomas Nelson.

Blanchard, Hodges and Hybeis, Bill. (1999). <u>Leadership by the Book</u>. New York: William Morrow and Co., Inc.

Blanchard, K. (1985). <u>Leadership and the One Minute Manager</u>. New York: William Morrow and Co., Inc.

Blanchard, Kenneth and Stoner, Jesse. (2003) <u>Full Steam Ahead!: Unleash the Power of Vision in Your Company and Your Life.</u> San Francisco: Berrett-Koehler.

Blanchard, Kenneth and McBride, Margret. (2003). <u>The One Minute Apology: A Powerful Way to Make Things Better.</u> New York: HarperCollins Publishers.

Blank, W. (2001). <u>The 108 Skills of Natural-Born Leaders</u>. New York: American Management Association.

Bonk, Kathy <u>et al</u>. (1999). <u>The Jossey-Bass Guide to Strategic Communications for Nonprofits</u>. San Francisco: Jossey-Bass Publishers.

Bossidy, Larry and Charan, Ram. (2004). <u>Confronting Reality: Doing What Matters to Get Things Right.</u> New York: Crown Business.

Bossidy, Larry, and Charan, Ram with Charles Burck. (2002). <u>The Discipline of Getting Things Done.</u> New York: Crown Business, Crown Publishing Group, Random House.

Cliffton, Donald O. and Nelson, Paula. (1996). <u>Soar With Your Strengths</u>. Princeton, NJ: Gallup Publications

Cain, Herman. (2000). <u>The CEO of Self</u>. Irving, TX: Tapestry Press

Cashman, K. (2000). <u>Leadership from the Inside Out</u>. Provo, UT: Executive Excellence Publishing.

Connellan, Thomas K. (2003). <u>Bringing out the Best in Others</u>. Austin: Bard Press.

Cook, Samuel DuBois. (2000). <u>Black Leadership for Social Change</u>. Westport, CT: Greenwood Press.

Covey, Stephen. (1992). <u>Principle-Centered Leadership</u>. New York: Fireside.

Covey, Stephen. (1990). <u>The Seven Habits of Highly Effective People</u>. New York: Simon & Schuster

Dees, J. Gregory <u>et al</u>. (2001). <u>Enterprising Nonprofits</u>. Somerset, NJ: John Wiley & Sons.

Dees, J. Gregory <u>et al</u>. (2002). <u>Strategic Tools for Social Entrepreneurs</u>. Somerset, NJ: John Wiley & Sons.

DePree, M. (1997). <u>Leadership Without Power</u>. Holland, MI: Shepherd Foundation.

Despain, James and Bodman, Jane. (2003). <u>And Dignity for All: Unlocking the Greatness through Values-Based Leadership.</u> Converse. Upper Saddle River, NJ: Financial Times Prentice Hall.

DeVries, M. (2001). <u>The Leadership Mystique--A User's Manual for the Human Enterprise</u>. New York: Financial Times Prentice Hall.

Drucker, Peter F. (1992). <u>Managing the Non-Profit Organization</u>. New York: Harper Business.

Emil, Angelica and Hyman, Vincent. (1997). <u>Coping With Cutbacks</u>. Saint Paul, MN: Amherst H. Wilder Foundation.

Fullan, Michael. (2001). <u>Leading Change</u>. San Francisco: Jossey-Bass.

Galford, Robert and Drapeau, Anne Seibold. (2003). <u>The Trusted Leader: Bringing out the Best in Your People and Your Company.</u> New York: The Free Press.

Gerber, Michael E. (2005). <u>E-Myth Mastery: The Seven Essential Disciplines for Building a World Class Company.</u> New York: Harper Collins Publishers, Inc.

Gerber, Robin. (2002). <u>Leadership the Eleanor Roosevelt Way</u>. New York: Prentice Hall Press.

Giuliani, Rudolph. (2002). <u>Leadership</u>. New York: Miramax.

Goldsmith, Marshall. (2003) <u>The Many Facets of Leadership.</u> Upper Saddle River, NJ: Financial Times Prentice Hall.

Goleman, Daniel <u>et al</u>. (2002). <u>Primal Leadership</u>. Boston: Harvard Business School Press.

<u>Harvard Business Review on Nonprofits.</u> (1999). Boston: Harvard Business School Press.

Hesselbein, Frances. (2002). <u>Hesselbein on Leadership</u>. San Franciso: Jossey-Bass

Hersey, Paul. (1985). <u>The Situational Leader</u>. New York: Warner Books

Hurd, Mark and Nyberg, Lars. (2004) <u>The Value Factor: How Global Leaders Use Information for Growth and Competitive Advantage.</u> Princeton, NJ: Bloomberg Press.

Joni, Saj-nicole. (2004) <u>The Third Opinion: How Successful Leaders Use Outside Insight to Create Superior Results.</u> New York: Portfolio--The Penguin Group.

Kotter, John P. (1996). <u>Leading Change</u>. Boston: Harvard Business School Press.

Kotter, John P. (1986). <u>Power and Influence</u>. New York: The Free Press

Kotter John P. (Ed.). (1999). <u>What Leaders Really Do</u>. Watertown, MA: Harvard Business School Press.

Kouzes, James M. and Posner, Barry Z. (2002). <u>The Leadership Challenge</u>. (3rd ed). San Francisco: Jossey-Bass.

Maxwell, John C. (2000). <u>Developing the Leader Within</u>. Nashville: Thomas Nelson Publishing.

Maxwell, John C. (1998). <u>The 21 Irrefutable Laws of Leadership</u>. Nashville: Thomas Nelson Publishing.

Maxwell, John C. (1998). <u>The 21 Most Powerful Minutes of a Leader's Day</u>. Nashville: Thomas Nelson Publishing.

Mittelstaedt, Robert, Jr. (2005). Will Your Next Mistake Be Fatal? Avoiding the Chain of Mistakes That Can Destroy Your Organization. Upper Saddle River, NJ: Wharton School Publishing.

McGinnis, Alan Loy. (1985). Bring Out the Best in People. Naples, FL: Augsburg Fortress Publishers

McRae-McMahon, Dorothy. (2001). Daring Leadership for the 21st Century. Sydney: ABC Books.

Munroe, Myles Dr. (1996). Maximizing Your Potential. Indianapolis: Destiny Image Publisher

Nanus, Burt and Dobbs, Stephen M. (1999). Leaders Who Make a Difference. San Francisco: Jossey-Bass Publishers.

Nelson, Bob and Economy, Peter. (2003). Managing for Dummies. (Second ed.) Indianapolis: Wiley Publishing , Inc.

Noonan, David. (2005). Aesop & the CEO: Powerful Insights from Aesop's Ancient Fables. Nashville: Thomas Nelson, Inc.

Operating Grants for Nonprofit Organizations. (2000). Phoenix: Oryx Press.

Ringer, Robert. (2004). To Be or Not To Be Intimidated? That Is the Question. New York: M. Evans and Company.

Robert III, Henry M. et al. (2000) Robert's Rules of Order (Newly Revised 10th ed). Cambridge, MA: Perseus Publishing.

Robbins, Harvey and Finley, Michael. (2004). The Accidental Leader. San Francisco: Jossey-Bass.

Ruiz, Don Miguel. (1997). The Four Agreements. San Rafael, CA: Amber Allen Publisher, Inc.

Secretan, Lance. (2004). Inspire! What Great Leaders Do. Hoboken, NJ: John Wiley & Sons.

Singh, D. (2000). Emotional Intelligence at Work. Howard Oaks, CA: Sage.

Tichy, Noel. (1999). The Leadership Engine. New York: HarperBusiness.

Tichy, Noel. (2004). The Cycle of Leadership: How Great Leaders Teach Their Companies to Win. New York: HarperBusiness.

Tisch, Jonathan M. (2004). The Power of We: Succeeding through Partnerships. Hoboken, NJ: John Wiley & Sons, Inc.

Walters, Ron. (1999). African American Leadership. Ithica, NY: SUNY Press.

Williams, Judith and Frohlinger, Carol. (2004). Her Place at the Table: A Woman's Guide to Negotiating: Five Key Challenges to Leadership Success. San Francisco: Jossey-Bass.

Williams, Terrie et al. (1994). The Personal Touch. New York: Time Warner Trade Publishing.

Wolf, Thomas. (1999). Managing a Nonprofit Organization in the Twenty-first Century. New York: Fireside.

GENERAL BUSINESS RESOURCES

WEB SITES OF GENERAL INTEREST

American Association of Minority Businesses
www.website1.com/aamb

Black Enterprise
www.blackenterprise.com

Minority Business Development Agency
www.mbda.gov

National Association for the Self-Employed
www.nase.org

National Association of Home-Based Businesses
www.usahomebusiness.com

National Business Incubation Association
www.nbia.gov

National Federation of Independent Business
www.nfibonline.com

SCORE (Service Corps of Retired Executives)
www.score.org

U.S. Small Business Administration and SBDCs (Small Business Development Centers)
www.sbaonline.sba.govT

The Kauffman Foundation
www.entreworld.com

Internal Revenue Service
www.irs.gov/businesses/small

INDEXES

Business Periodicals Index. New York: Wilson.
Subject index to articles in the fields of accounting, advertising, public relations, banking, economics, finance and investments, insurance, labor, management, marketing, and taxation. Also includes information on specific businesses, industries, and trades.

Readers' Guide to Periodical Literature. New York: Wilson.
Author and subject index to the contents of over 150 general and nontechnical magazines. A good starting point for finding information on a wide variety of topics.

.
Social Sciences and Humanities Index. Vols. 1-27, 1916-1974, formerly called;
International Index. Author and subject index to periodicals in the fields of anthropology, economics, environmental science, geography, law and criminology, political science, psychology, public administration, and sociology.

DICTIONARIES AND ENCYCLOPEDIAS

Middle Market Dictionary. New York: Dun and Bradstreet. Annual. This directory provides information about companies whose net worth ranges from $500,000 to $900,000 including utilities, transportation companies, banks and trust companies, stockbrokers, mutual and stock insurance companies, wholesalers, and retailers. The companies are listed alphabetically, geographically, and by product classification (S.I.C., Standard Industrial Classification).

Million Dollar Directory. New York: Dun and Bradstreet. Annual. Arranged as is Middle Market Directory. This compilation provides information about companies with a net worth of $1 million or more. It also contains a management directory that lists officers and directors and their affiliations.

Poor's Register of Corporations, Directors and Executives, United States and Canada. New York: Standard and Poor's Corporation. Annual. Volume I contains alphabetical listing of corporations with directors and executives. Volume 2 is a register of directors and executives of the companies listed in Volume 1. Volume 3 contains Standard Industrial Classification and geographical indexes. Supplements are issued in April, July, and October.

List of Small Business Investment Companies. Washington: U.S. Government Printing Office. Irregular.

National Minority Business Directory. Minneapolis: National Minority Business Directories. Annual. This specialized directory lists over 7,000 minority firms (50 percent or more owned by minority group members), classified by product. A cross-reference index aids in finding the appropriate classification. Computer disks are also available. Published by TRY US Resources, Inc. (612) 781-6819.

Thomas Register of American Manufacturers. New York: Thomas Publishing Company. Annual. Manufacturers are arranged according to product, and the manufacturers of each product are listed geographically. Alphabetical indexes to manufacturers, trade names, and specific products facilitate its use.

SPECIAL LISTS

Black Enterprise. New York, Monthly. The "top-100" black-owned or managed businesses that gross more than $1 million annually are listed in the June issue each year.

Forbes. New York. Semimonthly. The "Annual Report on American Industry" is in the first issue each year. It lists companies according to profitability, growth and pure stock gain over a five-year period. The "Annual Directory Issue" (May 15) ranks the top 500 corporations in sales, stock market value, assets, and profits.

Fortune. New York. Semimonthly. "The Directory of Largest Corporations" is an annual feature in several parts. The May issue lists the 500 largest U.S. industrial companies by sales. The June issue lists the second-largest 500 U.S. industrial companies. The July issue lists the largest nonindustrial corporations and the fifty largest companies in banking, life insurance, diversified financial services, retailing, transportation, and utilities.

Encyclopedia of Associations. Detroit: Gale Research. Revised approximately every two years. This classified directory lists over 12,000 organized groups. It lists for each, the address, phone number, chief official, a description, publications, and other pertinent information. The alphabetical and key-word index is helpful in locating an association if one does not know its exact name. Supplementary lists of new associations are issued quarterly.

The Foundation Directory. New York: Compiled by the Foundation Center and distributed by Columbia University Press, This directory lists foundations by state. Each entry includes the corporate name, address, purpose, activities, and pertinent financial data.

BIBLIOGRAPHIES AND GUIDES

Coman, Edwin T. Sources of Business Information. (rev. ed.), Berkeley and Los Angeles: University of California Press. The first four chapters of this guide deal with methodology and the range of business sources. The remaining chapters treat such specific fields as accounting, real estate and insurance, and management. Limited to American and Canadian sources, and a few from England.

Encyclopedia of Business Information Sources. 2 vols. Detroit: Gale. Volume I is organized alphabetically by topic, with sub-headings by type of source. Lists primary and secondary sources of information.

PERIODICALS

Academy of Management Journal. Tampa, FL Quarterly.

Accounting Review. Sarasota, FL: American Accounting Association. Quarterly.

Administrative Science Quarterly. Ithaca, NY: Cornell University Graduate School of Business and Public Administration. Quarterly.

Black Enterprise. New York. Monthly.

Business Week. New York: McGraw-Hill. Weekly.

Commerce America. Washington: U.S. Department of Commerce. Bi-weekly. Order from U.S. Government Printing Office.

Dun's Review. New York: Dun & Bradstreet. Monthly.

Federal Reserve Bulletin. Washington: U.S. Board of Governors of the Federal Reserve System. Monthly.

Forbes. New York. Semimonthly.

Fortune. New York, Semimonthly.

Harvard Business Review. Boston: Harvard University Graduate School of Business Administration. Monthly.

Industry Week. Cleveland, Ohio: Penton Publishing Company. Weekly.

Money. Chicago. Monthly.

Monthly Labor Review. Washington: U.S. Government Printing Office. Monthly

Nation's Business. Washington: Chamber of Commerce of the United States. Monthly.

Survey of Current Business. Washington: U.S. Department of Commerce. Order from U.S. Government Printing Office. Monthly. Supplemented weekly by Business Statistics.

Wall Street Journal. New York: Dow Jones. 5 issues per week.

NOTES

[1] Kenneth Lawyer and Clifford Baumback, How to Organize and Operate a Small Business, 6th Edition (Englewood Cliffs, NJ: Prentiuce Hall, 1979, p. 56.)

[2] Hal B. Pickel, "Personality and Success: An Evaluation of Personal Characteristics of Successful Small Business Managers," Small Business Research Series No. 4. Small Business Administration (Washington, DC: G.P.O.), 1964.

[3] Small Business Administration, "Keys to Business Success," Office of Management Assistance (1973), p. 37.

A BUSINESS OF YOUR OWN
Business Publications and Services for the Entrepreneurial Woman

"Our purpose is to assist the entrepreneurial woman in pulling together the intricate components necessary to make a small business a success!!!"

FACT SHEET

A BUSINESS OF YOUR OWN is a multifaceted service firm that specializes in business publications and services designed to assist women in starting and managing small businesses.

A BUSINESS OF YOUR OWN publishes information that inspires, motivates, educates, and helps the female entrepreneur grow and develop skills to manage a successful business. Our publications range from basic start-up manuals to detailed guide books for implementing and managing a specific business.

A BUSINESS OF YOUR OWN does more than just present the nuts and bolts of initiating a business between the covers of a manual. We are different because entrepreneurial women are different! We also offer strategy sessions, workshops, seminars, business development retreats, and much more.

ABOUT OUR COMPREHENSIVE START-UP MANUALS.......

The informational publications from *A BUSINESS OF YOUR OWN* reflect an enormous amount of in-depth research and the expertise of many noted professionals. Our comprehensive business start-up publications utilize a uniquely designed, step-by-step, hands-on approach to business formulation. Crucial business development and management information is provided in an easy-to-understand format, followed by questions for the entrepreneur to address. The summarization of the answers to these questions will enable entrepreneurially minded women in pulling together the major components of their business. Worksheets are provided for the purpose of providing assistance in preparing a business plan. All business start-up publications are designed so that upon completion, entrepreneurs will have a detailed business plan for their venture.

Our manuals are: *Currently researched *Informational *Practical *Systematic *Motivational
*Comprehensive *Easy to understand *Designed for the Entrepreneurial Woman

Additional Publications for the Entrepreneurial Woman

- Starting a Child Care Center $49.95
- Starting a Craft Business $49.95
- Starting a Flower and Gift Shop $49.95

Shipping and Handling Costs: $4.00/manual ▲ *Traditional Discounts Offered to the Trade.*

A BUSINESS OF YOUR OWN
P.O.B. 210662 ▪ Nashville, Tennessee 37221-0662
Phone: (615) 646-3708 ▪ Fax: (615) 662-8584
E-mail: Success@womaninbiz.com   Web site: www.abusinessofyourown.com